A Sufi Went to War

Shamcher Bryn Beorse

☙

THE SHAMCHER ARCHIVES
ALPHA GLYPH PUBLICATIONS

A Sufi Went to War

© 1979 Bryn Beorse and © 2022 The Shamcher Archives
Introduction © 2022 by Carol Sill
Cover Design: Diane Feught

All rights reserved. No part of this book may be reproduced or transmitted in any form or by any means, electronic or mechanical, including photocopying, recording, or by any information storage and retrieval system without express written permission from the publisher. Any unauthorized reprint or use of this material is prohibited.

ISBN: 978-1-988368-06-1

Alpha Glyph Publications - Salt Spring Island, BC Cannada
shamcher.substack.com

After one of Sufi Inayat's talks, a listener asked, "Should a Sufi be a pacifist?"

Said Inayat, "If people of goodwill lay down their arms today, they will be forced into war, forced to fight—not for their ideals but against them."

Two of his children shortly afterwards distinguished themselves in World War II. I went over the hill to serve, though pacifists screamed at me.

Contents

Introduction	1
Mein Kaiser Mein Kaiser	7
Geopolitik and Sufis	11
From Oceano to Elverum	20
The Huldre	29
The Phantom Sub	37
A Veritable Navy Goat	45
Stale Beer	53
The Finn, A Cunning Man is He	59
To Kidnap a Head of State	66
The Littlest Things	71
Over the Hill and Into the Fire	76
A Welcome Turned T E R R O R	81
Gore	83
Spies are Beautiful	88
I Conquer Bardenberg	92
Nothing Ever Happens Up There	101
That Coming War	107
I Shall Call Him Finn	116
Idiot's Delight	121
Peace Strikes	126
Epilogue	133
Appendix	135

INTRODUCTION

Born in Norway, in 1896, Shamcher Bryn Beorse lived through two World Wars. As a pupil of the great Sufi, Hazrat Inayat Khan in the 1920's, he attended Summerschools in Suresnes and was first active in the Sufi center in Christiania (now Oslo.) His work as an engineer and economist took him throughout the world, where he performed Universal Worship and encouraged Sufi activities wherever possible (or even impossible.) A spy in WWII, Shamcher volunteered for many dangerous missions, saying that at 44 he had lived his life, and the younger men should be given a chance to do the same. Settling in California after the war he wrote books on economics and worked on research for the promising OTEC system of benign solar power from the sea. With Sam Lewis and Paul Reps, Shamcher was one of the few original pupils of Inayat Khan in the Bay Area at that time. Shamcher always said he didn't believe in the hierarchical teacher/disciple relationship, yet he was devoted to the teachings and presence of Hazrat Inayat Khan his whole life, and had many loving students, often with widely divergent views and affiliations.

As a Sufi during WWII, he carried with him notes for his manuscript for *Man and This Mysterious Universe*, a book Inayat Khan had inspired him to write. It was his overview of the human condition, although he had touched on these topics in his previous economic surveys. After the war, he expanded his writings: presenting his experiences as novels or in non-fiction, applying his expertise in engineering and economics for the benefit of the world. All his books are wide-ranging and defy categories.

This volume, *A Sufi Went to War*, is an exception. In it, he narrows the field to focus entirely on accounting his wartime experiences. *A Sufi Went to War* is its original manuscript title, but it has also been known as "The Plot to Kidnap Hitler" or "May I Kidnap a Kidnapable Head of State."

In the first chapter, *Mein Kaiser, Mein Kaiser*, Shamcher introduces the obedience to a hierarchical regime that gave rise to Hitler and

WWII. His childhood contact with the Kaiser while aboard ship in Norway stayed with him, setting the stage for what was to follow, while revealing the German goals and methods to his nine-year-old mind. In the next chapter, *Geopolitik*, he shares later experiences with German bosses in Borneo, along with an account of adventures in Dayakland—including an out-of-body event. That time in Borneo introduced him to a German who would prove helpful to him in his wartime exploits. The 1930s found Shamcher in Berlin, running a successful translation business that was soon to be infiltrated by German government-appointed "associates."

Throughout the time leading up to the war, Shamcher crisscrossed the globe. In Chapter 3, *Oceano to Elverum*, he reveals the shift into war. From pro-Nazi Hollywood stars in New York and Los Angeles to Gavin Arthur's Hill House in Oceano, intimations of the need to fight for Norway soon plunged Shamcher from a cold war into a hot one. He sailed back to Norway via the Panama Canal, and joined the Norwegian underground for the Battle of Elverum.

His war experience had begun. The book now expands on specific aspects of his wartime, on land, sea and air, including spycraft at the highest level.

The fourth chapter, *The Huldre*, intersperses a mythic realm of old Norse folklore into the action, as Shamcher ski-guides British MI-5 friends to safety in Sweden. This chapter is followed by three sections in which he is followed and interrogated by the Gestapo: *The Phantom Sub* occurs on a Finnish ship, *A Veritable Navy Goat* turns the tables during Gestapo interrogations, and *Stale Beer* follows more such encounters.

In *The Finn, A Cunning Man is He*, Shamcher describes working in the Norwegian Underground, as well as travel from Sweden to Helsinki to New York. Central to the book is an outline of one of his most intense plans: *To Kidnap a Head of State*. In conjunction with German generals and various Allied espionage units, this plan was tragically stalled and then stopped at the top, by the US President. Here Shamcher laments the loss of a plan that would have saved the lives of so many who were killed as the war was allowed to continue to rage on.

The Littlest Things looks back from San Francisco to Norway and accounts the exploits of Tronstad and sabotage of the transport of heavy water from Norway to German atom bomb research.

In *Over the Hill and Into the Fire*, he moves from a desk in the Army to flight in the RAF, stealing supplies behind enemy lines and turning the tables once more on would-be captors. His tongue-in-cheek happy chapter, *A Welcome turned Terror,* is a lighthearted account of the liberation of Brussels, starkly followed by *Gore*, outlining the realities of German torture, as experienced by Count Stauffenberg, an anti-Nazi German. Torture was the real threat he faced as a spy every day. In *Spies are Beautiful*, he hails spies as great heroes of wartime, and outlines espionage, spy capture, rumours of his CIA connections.

With *I Conquer Bardenberg* the war comes close to the end, and here, with American GIs, while still in his RAF uniform, Shamcher fights on foot beside sympathetic German farmers to rout the last of the Nazis in Bardenberg. Air battle is described in *Nothing Ever Happens Up There*, flying with American B-24s over Germany.

Yet at the end of this war, intimations of a new war is coming. Shamcher went on a clandestine mission to Russia from Kirkenes in Norway, the closest town to the Russian border. In Chapter 17, this combined Russo-Norwegian effort revealed to him a new Russian effort toward *That Coming War*.

A dangerously misunderstood local hero is saved in *I Shall Call Him Finn*, when Shamcher and a head of the Underground find a way to release a Norwegian home front volunteer from overzealous post-war citizens.

In Chapter 19 is titled *Idiot's Delight*, as despite being called an idiot, Shamcher is appointed by Norway's Prime Minister to participate in the post-war economic rebuilding plan. *Peace Strikes* shows him finding his way in a post-war world. From LA to NY to Spain to NY to Oslo, from hitch-hiker to squatter in the Stortinget building of the Norwegian Congress, he finally settled in a New York brownstone, to begin a new life as an American.

This volume holds some of Shamcher's history and the stories of others who fought so we could take for granted the freedom that was threatened in the turmoil of twentieth century wartime. It is not a full account, but only taps lightly on the surface of the wartime lessons in life. In many of his other books, Shamcher retells or refers to some of these wartime exploits. Included in the Appendix here is the chapter *War*, from *Every Willing Hand*.

In his book, *Fairy Tales are True*, Shamcher's description of returning to the dunes of Oceano reveals the coarse and insouciant post-war attitude as the two Army Intelligence buddies rename an artist's paintings after the war. (The character, Dreamwood, was based on the Dunite artist Elwood Decker.)

> But finally, the War was finished and I was free to return to the dunes. I invited a friend and fellow from Army Intelligence, Rene, and the both of us hurried across the Atlantic and across the country to the dunes. Never, in my thoughts during the years I was away, had I considered the possibility of change. I had gone on assuming that the same people would still be there when I returned, in the same setting. Only as we were leaving Oceano and beginning the walk across the dunes, did the fear and the realization of the possibility of change strike me.
>
> But the same cranes and storks were still selecting their menus with majestic disdain from the shallow creek which still wandered coolly among the tall reeds and pussy willows between banks covered with bursts of brightly-colored flowers. A shimmering, subtropic haze hung overhead and beyond the expanse of yellow sand was the sapphire-blue ocean.
>
> This was my return. I looked aside at Rene. The beauty was not all in my own eyes. There was an urgency about him and, when we turned south along the beach, he rushed along the wet sand, past the serenely-staring pelicans. Then, when we turned back inland, his long legs outran me completely. He turned and gave me a grateful look from the point where the greenery sprang up from the sand and then he hurried on, heading right for Dreamwood's cabin as if he had known this path all his life.
>
> Dreamwood was not at home, but before he left, he had put

his paintings out to take the sun and I found Rene admiring them as I came panting up.

"These are fabulous," he said. "But, of course, the titles must be changed."

"Of course," I said, looking once more at the crimson splotch entitled *All beauty begins at the vanishing point of the seeming-self.*

"The man's a great artist, except with words," said Rene. "It's our duty as officers and gentlemen to help him."

We set about writing out new titles on little bits of paper which we fastened with pins above the old so that our changes were not irreversible. The crimson blotch we called, *Atom bombs play baseball*. A monumental canvas featuring dark, amorphous bodies entangled in a bitter struggle was titled by Dreamwood, *Astral studies from the Atman plane*. We retitled it, *The Battle of the Bulges*.

[...Dreamwood returned...]

When he reached his cabin, his meditation did not prevent him from seeing the new names we had put on his paintings. He looked at them, one by one, and then fixed Rene with a look so fixed and angry that it made my stomach feel hollow. Rene answered him with a grin which just intensified the look on Dreamwood's face.

"Don't be angry," I said to Dreamwood. "It was all in fun. They can be taken off."

I knelt and pulled off a couple of the scraps of paper. Dreamwood looked at me with a look which was almost friendly and then turned his fixed, hurt look back on Rene.

...

A Sufi Went to War is an outline of wartime experience that encompasses land, sea, and air. Shamcher, as a Sufi, faced it all head on. He threw himself fully and wholeheartedly into the cause, whatever the risks may have been. He was driven by the cause, following and relying upon his intuition and love of humanity to help create a better world for the future.

Carol Sill, Salt Spring Island, 2022

Chapter 1

Mein Kaiser, Mein Kaiser

Is life mapped out for one at the age of nine? That was when I met the Kaiser and had my first inkling of German goals and methods, which reappeared in a cruder pattern in a later German leader whom I fought as a simple soldier who "does the hacking" as Leo Tolstoy put it in *War and Peace*.

Seldom is the hacking soldier permitted to plan (let alone plan his own hacking) but brilliant British officers took on my clumsy plans and wishes, forged them into such elegant verbiage that they were presented—and enthusiastically accepted by Britain's top leadership—to be shot down from across the Atlantic.

Yes, I knew Germans from my ninth year. This all began in 1905. I was the youngest crewmember on S/S Hydrograph, an 80 ton service vessel of the Royal Norwegian Navy. I had just received my papers as an Ordinary Seaman, not yet ablebodied.

I leaned over the railing and looked at the jet black side of the trim official ship, and at the yellow band painted all around her which gave her distinction. I looked up at the bridge where my father, pencil in mouth, looked fiercely at the surrounding mountains through an instrument that would locate the place we now occupied in this wild sanctuary, a Navy hideout, a white, empty space on any official map. Then I looked at those mountains, or between them, and saw masts. I pointed and shouted. My father lowered his instrument and looked. Then he frowned. His face tightened. Without a word he pushed down the signal lever to full speed ahead.

It was always a thrill to watch my father maneuver the small steamer in and out of narrow passages, and particularly when he was angry. He was angry now. He knew the Norwegian coast better than any other man: he had mapped it. Now he steamed full speed against the solid rock—until the rock opened and a tiny slit permitted entry of the Hydrograph. What magic! By such feats, followed in too-rapid-succession to be counted, a small but representative vessel entered a wide bay in which was a pure white palace-on-the-sea snuggling against an overhung mountainside.

Hydrograph's signal lamp blinked: "... I am coming aboard, as representative of the Royal Norwegian Navy."

A boat was lowered. I looked at my father. He read my burning desire. "All right. You saw her first. Come along!"

What a sailor-like decision. A mere landlubber would never have thought of bringing along a nine-year-old on such a mission, not to a sailor, whose life depends on sharp eyes and alert minds; to him age does not matter, only sharp eyes and alert minds.

At the sumptuous yacht a boarding ladder was obligingly lowered. There isn't much a visitor in a secret Navy haven can do when hailed by the host Navy. The visit must be accepted.

I scrambled up behind my father. A lieutenant at the upper landing saluted smartly. My father asked to be taken to the bridge. There, a lean weatherbeaten Admiral leaned down to listen to a short man, also in Admiral's uniform, plus some extras.

I was fascinated by this little man. He was almost down to my size, so I could view him almost like an equal, and I compared him with some boys I had known. His eyes flicked and blazed like a bully-boy's who bamboozles and browbeats his playmates—until he meets one stronger. Then he pouts.

When I look back at this scene now, at that wiser, taller admiral leaning down and kowtowing to the sputtering stream of words in front of him, how much could I have sensed or glimpsed? Had this helped me evaluate that German leader 35 years later, whom I so narrowly missed expatriating?

My father hovered over this willful child, interrupting his stream of words, "Your Majesty is in secret Norwegian waters. I shall take your ship out."

The Kaiser looked up, pouting a little at the commanding tone of voice of the Royal Norwegian Navy. My father already had his hand on the engine telegraph.

"Your Majesty, do you wish me to take over your ship or will you leave it in command of an officer I shall instruct?"

The Kaiser's eyes flashed and flicked. He seemed to reach for a victory but finally chose surrender, "Admiral Schultze, we are in the benevolent hands of a mighty Navy. Obey her orders! Carry on!"

The Kaiser now tried a new trick. He came over and stroked my golden locks, then turned to my father, "What a fine little Viking you have here!"

I felt like smacking the Kaiser on the nose. Daddy's stone face did not budge but he ordered increased speed that made the big ship quiver and tremble as it shot in and out of the narrowest channels. The Kaiser and his Admiral held their breath.

Just then, as the two were putty in my father's hands, he sternly demanded to see all the charts they had of this area. The Kaiser nodded at Admiral Schultze, who responded with a furious stare at his Kaiser. The Kaiser softened under that stare and looked pleadingly at my father who repeated, more sternly than before, "The charts, please, all of them!"

The Kaiser spoke gently to Admiral Schultze, "Admiral, the charts?"

The Admiral tried his serious stare again. It did not prevail. He finally had to yield and talk down a chute, and a few minutes later a studious-looking officer appeared with charts under his arm. The Kaiser presented, "Captain Berndt, our navigation wizard!"

While keeping track of the ship's movements, my father scrutinized the charts. Then he thrust a fierce glance at Captain Berndt, "Captain, you must have more charts of this area!"

The Captain did not answer. He looked pleadingly at his Kaiser, who said, "Well, Captain?"

"Captain Berndt," said my father—and there was thunder in him now—"It is it imperative that you submit every chart you have of this area, before I can clear this ship for further travel!"

"Well, Captain Berndt," said the Kaiser, "Bring all you have, all!"

The German captain looked furiously at his supreme commander, then saluted, turned and tramped off, shaking his head. We could hear him mutter, "Mein Kaiser, Mein Kaiser!"

Seconds and minutes ticked by but Captain Berndt did not come back. My father responded by more frenzied speed, more last-minute escapes from crashes, until the nervous wreck of a Kaiser and Emperor screamed for his navigation wizard. He finally returned. Whether the formidable bundle he now carried under his arm was all he had or he had managed to copy them 40 years before the Xerox machine was invented is anybody's guess, but you have to draw the line somewhere, and my father accepted the offering and shoved it into a huge inner pocket of his jacket so he looked like a veritable monster.

Then he addressed the Kaiser, "I am obliged to keep these. Your majesty may at anytime get in touch with the foreign service of the Royal Norwegian Government should you have any doubt or complaint in the matter."

Captain Berndt shook his head again. He didn't say it aloud this time, but one could almost hear his silent commiserations, "Mein Kaiser, Mein Kaiser!"

The ship rushed right against a rock. The Kaiser's eyes widened, Admiral Schultze's frowns deepened and Captain Berndt stopped his headshaking and stared. The rock opened. The big ship slid through. Leaning over the railing one could almost touch rock. A moment later we found ourselves in a broad and busy thoroughfare. Ships of all sizes, types and of many nations came and went and paid us scant attention. We were outside the Navy sanctum.

By the time the ultimate purpose of the Kaiser's visit to the Royal Norwegian Navy sanctuary became fully revealed to me, I had grown to be a man.

Chapter 2

Geopolitik and Sufis

Geopolitik is the word that describes and explains the Germans. It means looking at the greater area, the same idea that was expressed in the Common Market, earlier in the United States, and the British Commonwealth of Nations, and, in a smaller area of the Swiss confederacy.

A crucial question once was: when a German looked at the territory within Germany's borders, and then beyond, to Denmark, Norway, Sweden and then felt that these areas belonged geopolitically with Germany rather than England—what did he want to do about it?

Great German statesmen, such as Frederick the Great, von Motke, and von Bismarck, had patience, never even hinting a solution against the wishes of the local people. Against these were pitted a childish man like Kaiser Wilhelm II, the despair of Bismarck and of the suave, sophisticated General Staff, and later Hitler, who was exploited by these generals as a temporary rabble-rouser—to be disposed of at the proper time in order to install suave General von Schleicher as the leader of Germany and its geopolitik. But Goering along with other Hitler aides discovered the army plot and shot von Schleicher in his home, before the eyes of his wife.

Kaiser Wilhelm II and Hitler both had a simplistic view of the world as it existed and how to make it over. They never understood the subtle and free relationship between England and the Scandinavian countries. They considered Norway a pitiable vassal under England, ready to be made a less pitiable vassal under Germany. If a few stubborn Norwegians had to be punished and, during the Hitler era, even whipped on their bare bottoms, to be brought in line and scare others from resisting, then that was seen as a small price to pay for a great international favor.

When the Kaiser was defeated in World War I, and completed his life chopping wood in Holland, the Germans reacted strongly against previous imperial policies. A truly democratic, humanized Weimar Republic was established, guided by the mature policies of such leaders as Walter Rathenau, Stressemann, Bruning and others. The recurrence of wild dreams, culminating in the Hitler regime, was caused in part by American and British ignorance. Reparations were demanded from the Germans, not in German goods and services, which were all they had as payment, but in dollars or pounds, which the Germans could obtain only by selling German goods to England or America, and which these nations refused to accept. Many Germans starved outright and a starving man will try anything.

But Kaiser Wilhelm did not have this excuse. Germany was rich and proud and arrogant when he came to power. His excursions to the Norwegian fjords and sanctuaries were for acquainting himself with this great and exciting potential—elbow room for a new, great German fleet of the sea and—might he be permitted to dream—a German air arm! And he hoped to win many Norwegians as personal friends, or at least admirers, so that the takeover would be gentle and a shoo-in.

There were preparations of a different kind. An agent of the Kaiser bought an island on the Oslo Fjord. It was said to be for a chicken farm. A solid concrete floor was provided for the coops, so solid, we found, that it would support huge German howitzers that could command the entire fjord leading in from the Skagerrak and, vice versa, could be directed at the city of Oslo. As Winston Churchill quipped, on another occasion, "Some chicken."

Berlin, a huge passenger ship in peacetime, an auxiliary cruiser during World War I, sought refuge from British warships in the fjord leading into Trondheim, Norway's ancient capital and seat of an engineering university employing two German professors, Wirtz and Matzinger. The ship sneaked past Agdenes Fort under cover of night and greeted Trondheim with a 21 gun salute, during which lively signaling was observed between the window in Professor Wirtz's house and the ship. Among critics to this insult to Norwegian security, Professor Matzinger was the most outspoken—a Molkte-Bismarck-Rathenauer type of German.

I was 18 then, twice the age when I had met the Kaiser and could think of no better way to react to German leadership at the time than to enlist with the French. They turned me down. I joined an officers' training course, so tough that the commanding officer prompted us with the point of his saber at our behinds when we lagged at marches. Peace arrived and delayed the utilization of our fiercely trained men until World War II.

Meanwhile, an engineer and officer, though hardly yet a gentleman, I shipped out to Dutch East India (now Indonesia). For the first few months I was the houseguest of my German boss. His table abounded in salty wurst. Politely I helped myself modestly to some of this throat-strangling stuff. It wasn't enough.

Mr. Blank looked at me sorrowfully, "Herr Bjorset, Sie sind kein grossen freund von wurst!"

It was never the same between us after that. I felt I must leave his home. But I had great respect for him as an honest, hard-working and hard-eating German, and not the dictator type but the type who bows before dictators as so many Germans did. This seems to be the reason why they did not throw out Hitler.

I don't know if it was a sausage incident or other matters that made Mr. Blank feel my psyche needed a stiffener. When the Dutch Inspector General came on a visit Mr. Blank told him I was working hard but obviously out of sorts, since I hadn't made liaison with a single native woman. Perhaps I didn't like some Malays, so would the Inspector General please see about sending out some Javanese beauty?

The Inspector General looked at me, "Affirmative?"

I shook my head, "Negative."

Then Mr. Blank had an inspiration. Past our village named Kandangan flowed the dirty Amandit River and this was the same river from which the irrigation water was taken. So he wanted to know about its sources and upper run, to determine its reliability as a water source, year-round. This perfectly legitimate desire from an irrigation engineer fitted my ambition as an adventurer. This is what Mr. Blank's brain and thought wiggles had figured out.

Sources and upper reaches of the Amandit River were situated in headhunter land, the mountains of the Dayaks. In the lower regions of this area only two white men had ever ventured, the Dutch tax collector and the Controller. They had been protected by twelve Malay policemen. Malays are not the best protectors among Dayaks who hate Malay worse than they do whites. The white men had never returned, nor had any of the Malay policemen. They were assumed now to adorn some Dayak chief's shrunk head collection.

In the upper regions of this area where the sources of the Amandit River would have to be sought, no point man for Malay had ever ventured. This is where I was now allowed to go. Mr. Blank had hit the nail on the head with me.

In the lower region with the tax collector's head may have been shrunk, I had a slight adventure the first night, while sleeping on a cot under a roof and with no walls. I left my body and floated under the ceiling, looking down on myself with some concern, for the native chief was approaching with a drawn sword. I tried to wake me up but insouciantly I slept on, until the very last-minute, when I rose from the bed, composed by instructions from the part of me floating above, and approached the approaching chief who bowed ceremoniously and said he had come to protect me from any unforeseen act by any unforeseen adversary. For this thoughtful kindness I thanked him profusely, adding that it would not really be necessary since my gun, which I always carried with me, was so constructed that it automatically shot anyone who attacked me. Well, I don't really know if I succeeded in conveying this exact message to the chief in my halting Malay, which language he hated anyway, and probably didn't understand very well, though something must have seeped through for I was spared any nightly approaches anywhere along the trail. Contributing to the state of affairs was also my rising prestige: it was realized that I was no tax collector but, with my rain meters, my interest in watercourses and sources, I was no doubt an assistant of the Great Rain God himself.

I don't know if Herr Blank had counted on my committing myself to a Dayak woman and had sent me along for this explicit purpose. I must say that these statuesque mountain women appealed to me, thrilled me, could have seduced me without really trying, but the wry smile of a voluptuous wife of the Chief who wanted to cut my head off was hardly in the way of invitation. I wasn't sure whether she was annoyed that her husband hadn't succeeded or whether she was enjoying my hungry look, but I would not be the one to provide her worthy chief-husband with a new and real reason to use his sword on me.

More restraint and resolve was required of me to resist the temptation trust at me at the fifth village I visited. There, after a luscious evening meal, a naked young girl, came up to me all by herself, smiling her giveaway, and the Medicine Man and the Chief both nodded their approval.

I stroked the girl's shining hair and walked her back to her parents. I was not going to risk my young life making music with a girl whose background and standards I knew so little about. I might so easily end up a head shorter and, as far as I knew, I didn't own more than one usable head. I have been worried ever since whether the Taywany tribe of the Dayaks believe, after this halfway performance of mine, that stroking a girl's hair is all a white man knows about romance and love.

I returned to the village of Kendangan and my boss, with a comprehensive concept of the sources and upper regions of the Amandit River, and with a heartburn for my Dayak woman whom I had left with softly stroked hair.

Upon my return I found our engineering staff augmented with Freiherr von Bundschu, a German nobleman with no more taste for wurst than myself (showing one should never judge a whole nation on wurst alone) and a monocle fastened with a broad black band. Freiherr von Bundschu got along splendidly with me, much better than with his compatriot, boss Blank. As we entered the irrigation offices together one morning, looking over the Malay draftsmen sitting crosslegged, bent over their drawing boards, the Freiherr coughed, "Ahem, do not these men rise and salute when we enter?"

Pringovardia, the Javanese supervisor, knew German and winked at me, "To an engineer, may I arrange a tour of the irrigation works, showing them to the new engineer?"

"Good idea, Pringo, go ahead."

Pringo conducted this tour across a number of bamboo footbridges, each consisting of just one slim, rickety bamboo beam that swayed and shook as you probed your way across. In the middle, where the shaking and the swaying were at their worst, a gray head appeared underneath, the head of a sleepy alligator slowly opening its huge jaws in anticipation.

The Freiherr lost his monocle in the middle of the first bridge. It fell to the full length of the black band, then swayed. This experience seems to have changed the Freiherr's attitude toward the Malay draftsmen and their rising or not rising when we engineers entered. He never mentioned it again. The idea seemed to have disappeared from his mind, a development obviously foreseen by Pringovardia when he concocted his foot-bridge-crossing itinerary.

Something much different worried this German nobleman now, and also Mr. Blank, the boss. They talked together more and more about Germany's future, a comeback of a strong and mighty Germany that would rule the world. From then on a disagreement developed: Blank wanted a poor man's son to lead Germany, one who had felt poverty. The noblemen wanted a sophisticated well-educated, upper-class dandy, preferably an army officer. At this point, seething passion reigned. Blank banged his fist on the table. Bundschu eyed him coldly.

Finally Blank took the only sensible way out: a vacation. It was the first he had had in many years. I was put in charge. Blank subjected me to intensive briefings. Halfway through one of them he suddenly stopped, obviously embarrassed, and looked at me sorrowfully, "There is the matter of the payroll."

"Yes?"

"160,000 guilders in small notes by riverboat from Bandjermassin every week."

"Fine"

Now he scrutinized me sternly, "You would not run away with that money, would you?"

I was stunned. What horrible things had I done to evoke such suspicions? My boss looked me over again with a searching and then less and less accusing glance, and said, "No, I think not. Not for 160,000. If it had been a million that would have made it another matter."

Another accusation, I realized it was not. In the eyes of this particular beholder it was appreciation, bordering on flattery. But I could not help but asking, "Why would it have been another matter if it has been a million?"

Mr. Blank shrugged, "Everyone has his price."

I repeated the story to the Freiherr to see if I had discovered a national German trait. The Freiherr's words reassured me that I had not. "Honor cannot be bought for billions."

And it was this man, Freiherr von Bundschu, who was to save my life when, twenty years later, I was captured doing the wrong things during the Nazi occupation of Norway.

My out-of-the-body dream experience in Dayakland had revived my taste for yoga which I had studied since my 16th year. I decided to leave my job in Borneo and crisscross India in search of a worthy teacher. He did not appear in India but on my doorstep, when I returned to my home in Oslo. A Hindu musician and mystic, Inayat Khan, asked me to translate his talks at the Oslo University and I became his pupil. He called himself a Sufi.

Sufis and yogis seem to me now to have been the source of all religions and most science, though these religions and sciences generally deteriorated into rigid mind concepts from the subtle, flowing all-embracing streams of wisdom and the sentiments of vital Sufis and yogis. An example is the confusion of every religion and most sciences in the face of military service. After one of Sufi Inayat's talks, a listener asked, "Should a Sufi be a pacifist?"

Said Inayat, "If people of goodwill lay down their arms today, they will be forced into war, forced to fight—not for their ideals but against them."

Two of his children shortly afterwards distinguished themselves in World War II. I went over the hill to serve, though pacifists screamed at me.

I saw a World War II foreshadowed plan, in Berlin in the 30s. I built a business, Orientalistengemeinschaft, an association of engineers and linguists with experience in the Orient. Ahmed, my Turkish friend and interpreter, his German wife slave Metha, Hindus, Chinese, Japanese, Malays, Vietnamese and Javanese shared the worries and the profits. One typical day we received a rush call for a Chinese language expert. Our expert was notified by phone but as soon as he was on his way, out of reach, the order was canceled. I told him the bad news when he arrived, and added that he would be paid, from the organization's funds, not merely for his travel expenses and also for his time.

The energetic young scholar was not dismayed at all. "Excellent!" he jubilated, "and in that case, I insist on doing something for you in return. I will give you full value for your payment: I shall spend the next and coming hour teaching you Chinese!"

I thought of a thousand excuses but none came forth for my energetic Chinese scholar didn't give me a chance. He propounded sounds and grimaces the likes of which I had never before heard or seen, then forced me to repeat, or try to. That hour was the hardest in my life. My Chinese teacher left to me only after he had become thoroughly convinced that I had no more money to pay for Chinese classes.

But it was my German associates who really floored me. Well, why did I have German associates in the first place? Because a new, Nazi-inspired law said that a foreigner, even a Norwegian though belonging to the super-race, had to have a genuine German associate in order to conduct business in Germany. The authorities were even helpful enough to suggest who. This is how Herr Heinrich Hoffman came to be my associate.

Heinrich Hoffman had the loudest voice. And he so enjoyed using it. Once I had ordered some printed matter and when it didn't arrive on time I had a friendly discussion with the printing firm about a later delivery. Heinrich Hoffman listened to this, then bellowed, "Give me the phone!"

He spewed into that instrument a cacophony of shrieks that must have broken eardrums at the receiving station. They certainly broke mine. After the performance he looked at me as Caruso must have looked at his fans, after his glass-shattering performance.

Heinrich Hoffman's wrath was to be used for a more profitable purpose: backed by ever new laws and more shrieks he bore down upon me until he had the business, the money I had stuck into it, the reputation we had acquired, and I had to leave. I heard recently he was still doing fine. Orientalistengemeinschaft!

If it hadn't been for Friedel and Liza, the whole thing wouldn't have been worthwhile. Friedel was my night girl and Liza was my day girl. In prewar Germany these were the proper things to have: a night girl and a day girl. Liza was the daughter of the Berlin police chief. This fact carried many favors. But Liza carried the greatest.

Chapter 3

From Oceano to Elverum

America is the great equalizer. German descendents and even immigrants ceased to be Germans and become such fervent Americans that a General Eisenhower wholeheartedly carried the American banner fighting messianic German racists. One who has known Germans in Germany stands amazed before this complete American conversion. Adolf Hitler boasted Blut Und Boden, but his "blood and soil" didn't do for his people what mere ideas did for the miracle that became America.

I had my first look at America during a routine business trip that became interspersed with adventures that made me wonder whether I ought not to blush. I attended a reception in Manhattan arranged by the Association of Motion Picture Producers to acquaint foreign correspondents with a selection of American female movie stars. I had no better excuse for my presence than having been, nine years ago, a worse than mediocre editor of a student sheet.

The reception hall was magnificent; the lights subdued—to mellow or to inflame the ardor of the visitors? A voluptuous number, whose name shall be guarded with my very life, lifted her glass and looked be deeply in the eyes, "Meet me on the coast...."

Two days and three nights I drove, without stop, in a state of total emblazonment and was awarded with an invitation to a party, and that was all. I pondered, in the night, my ineptness, my lack of education: did I not drink enough, or smoke the right brands, or did my eyes speak too much emotional hunger? I had come a long way and tried my luck with the German-born producer's daughter, who raved about the eruptive syntax of the Teutons, the only lingo that could orate the explosive ecstasies of carnal crescendos. Being cognizant of this Teutonic syntax, I reasoned there might be a promise here. Before I was to try out this yet unproven scientific hypothesis, already rocking in my fantasy upon mighty waves of passion, she fumbling late and differed to make me reveal the departure time and route of the ship to cross the Atlantic, facing German submarines. Catharina the Great of Russia had her lovers butchered. This German maiden may have felt a submarine would do it.

That night she and I were in a giant party, a huge place dotted with tables, like a restaurant, though it wasn't. What was it? Affluence has its inscrutable outlets. I didn't think I needed to be nailed down to a German hostess playing with submarines, so I rose and walked around. From a large table came a voice like tinkling bells, "Who are you?"

I was stunned. The voice came from the greatest of the great at that time, a queen who could command any man or beast and, feeling nothing less worthy of her, I responded, humbly, "The Prince of the North Pole." Thoughtfully, I added, "And who are you?"

That question was a bomb, for who wouldn't know who she was? So modulated peels of laughter rewarded me, and she replied, "Oh, at present I am not sure but once upon a time I was in elevator girl back in Rockefeller Center."

"And did you like that better than what you are not so sure you are now?"

"Well, my Prince, the elevator job was uplifting."

At this point our intercourse was brutally interrupted by an apelike man rising from her table, taking a firm hold of her hips and turning her away from me, "That is enough."

Which move caused me to circle around so I again faced my queen, "Princess, is that man annoying you, or am I?"

Her eyelids clipped and her lovely voice was imploring, "Oh oh my gallant prince, free me from my monstrous agent and slave driver...."

The following afternoon, as she was driving down the Sunset Strip in her antique flat-windshielded European model, she saw me, waved and drove right into a telephone pole. Ever since I have thought that this was the height of consideration of a movie star for her devoted fan.

That night, back in the throes of Teutonic verbiage, there was a new note, impelling, amazing, disgusting. This lovely, intelligent, voluptuous, stretching, irresistible amazon now chattered away with clichés snatched from the cheapest Hitler propaganda, extolling that "great savior of Germany and the world" who would have sickened her if she had ever set eyes on him. All the while she looked searchingly, beseechingly at me, hoping for approval, nay, enthusiasm. When neither came, she launched into such a fierce curiosity about what ship I would take out of New York and when, that I made up a carefully structured story of an assumed departure and that same night repeated the story to certain authorities. Whether they set out to meet and trap whatever subs would be after my fiction ship I do not know, but the lady killed herself.

Should I be sorry? I have saved many lives of those who resisted the tyrant, and I may have killed some who served the tyrant and would have killed us if they had lived.

The lady who left this world had taught me a little about the fascination men and women could feel for a scatterbrain they did not know. I began to wonder and plan how to render this scatterbrain harmless. And with that, I felt a tugging at the heart roots: I must be in this war, I must play this game. My first step was not even impressive. I moved from the city of sin to the winds and salts of Oceano, the tiniest village, in a land of ocean spray and desert. I needed the fresh and lonely space, to think and ponder. There aren't any stars at Oceano except a few hardy ones who chase each other across the lonely desert and play lustful Adam and Eve, except that no fig leaves can be found, hardly even an apple. The long nights I spent at Gavin Arthur's Hill House listening to Gavin's and Esther's premonitions, voiced in chorus with the radio, all announcing that Hitler's next move would be into—Norway!

These words stuck. I knew there was something rotten about my cheap adventuring while the world was burning. It had weighed on my mind. Now I saw: it was time to use my know-how. My old Dodge breathed its last in a frantic run to San Pedro. I was still cheap enough to try for a free ride and after having bombarded the skipper of Emma Bakke with all my qualities, such as having bested the German Kaiser, and having had seaman papers at age 9, he nodded quietly, "Enjoyed your talk, but it wasn't necessary. Two men ran away here in San Pedro to try their tricks with the movie starlets, so we'd have had to take you on regardless."

In the big lake at highest point in the Panama Canal we ignorant Norwegian sailors dived and swam, laughing at the Captain's wild waving, until we finally came aboard and he told us about the lake alligators. "If it's adventure you're after, why not wait till the Atlantic!"

From the Canal outlet on we were at war, for the first time. My cold war with the Germans had plunged into a hot one. It gave me a tingling feeling of value and sense.

In New York we joined a convoy, which carried us about one third across. Then we were left alone until nearing the Irish coast. That's how it was done this early in the war, January 1940. Nearing the Irish coast however, we didn't find the convoy supposed to be there. Instead we picked up an SOS from a Finnish ship dead ahead which had just been torpedoed. So, surely we would be the next victim. Hmmm. This was not the way I had figured my first encounter with my German adversary in this war that had just become hot: an old tramp with a single cannon against a German racer sub. But we took it in stride, all but Olav, 16-year-old cabin boy, who sobbed disconsolately, "And I, who have never had a woman, and now I shall never have one—ever!"

The bosun's mate, who on a Norwegian freighter is a worse taskmaster than Beelzebub, now became a slobbering mother-father-consoler, "Olav, boy, don't you worry. We'll all be rowing in to Glasgow town and by golly will we show those Scots some who can row! And then I shall personally see to it that you shall have the fairest lass in that Glasgow town."

Olav looked up and dried his tears, "But will I get wet first?"

"No!" I thundered, more for stiffening my own psyche than for Olav's sake, "for I am on my way back to Norway to fight those #$$#@XX#, and I'm not about to take any funny business from them here in this wetwater."

An apparently useless bravado but, so it was to be! We sailed into Glasgow, no wetter than any other seamen. The sub didn't find us.

The immigration watchers and field security police in Glasgow had a ball, suspecting and harassing the sailors who had risked their lives bringing grain and fruits and egg powder to them and their children but after weeks of incredible questioning and retention of two suitcases full of private papers, I finally made it by air to beleaguered Norway. The very room where I had lived in my father's house, which had been sold years ago, was still free and for rent.

Was it two or three mornings later that a dinosaur wailed to hurried clouds rushing past a disturbed moon? Or was it not a dinosaur but an air raid siren? And not just testing or drill this time, but the real thing? Inside some of those clouds drifting past the moon's face were there not solid aircraft of a foreign model?

My landlady, the wife of the quiet insurance man who had bought my father's house, knocked on my door and whined, "Mr. Bjorset, Mr. Bjorset, something terrible must have happened and I believe it is war!"

So it had come, at last, and not only a sea encounter this time but actual war on Norway's own soil. This required action; I dressed, put on my overcoat, packed my cork hat on top of me, stuck my six-shooter in my pocket. Thus equipped, I walked out in the early morning to meet and deal with the invader.

The way out from that house to anywhere in the world was by electric train and this morning the train wasn't running so we walked, all of us who have gone out to act, along the tracks to Majorstuen, and there we followed the track underground to National Theatret. Coming up from that underground station, the only one in Oslo at the time, I saw a group of officer cadets running. The running looked purposeful. Besides, officer candidates might have an inkling of why they were running, where to, and for what reason. Taking a chance that all of these assumptions stuck, I joined them.

Their goal, it turned out, was Akershus Fort, an old dummy fort. My closest co-runners advised me that this was where the Germans had established their headquarters. Well, this might have been called an understatement since the Germans soon were to prove themselves experts in headquarters establishing. After a month, they had at least twenty, and thereupon the number grew by leaps and bounds. By war's end nobody knew how many. It was probably top-secret.

A large and threatening crowd had gathered before the big wrought iron gates of the fort. Inside German soldiers and Norwegian police were milling around, casting nervous glances at the crowd outside. The officer cadets and I went in search of appropriate timber to crash the gates.

When we returned, carrying between us a giant tree and rushing towards the locked iron gate, three Norwegian policemen waved desperately at me, probably feeling a man in a cork hat must have some kind of brain underneath it. For a moment I left my tree-carrying team and sidled up to the gate. The three policemen rasped, with their hands to their chins (I think they thought they were whispering): "If you guys want to fight, don't do it here, where you'll be mowed down like chicken. Go join the Norwegian forces north of Oslo…"

"Where!?" came my rasping reply, echoed by a hundred other rasping voices who had completely abandoned the huge tree now plunked down in the middle of the yard. The policemen responded, "Elverum!"

The next instant the place before the gates was wiped clean except for a huge tree that nobody cared about anymore and which would block German entries and exits for a period and in a manner which we contemplated with some satisfaction. Our more serious concern was how to get through the military cordon around Oslo. Hiking? Sneaking? Skiing? Bicycling? Trucking? Or the good old railroad? We discussed in the streets and in our homes, some in the Grand, a superbar, over a beer. The latter were immortalized by Leland Stowe who just been dropped into the same superbar and, not a linguist, promptly wired home, "The Norwegians accept the German invaders smilingly, over their beer."

It was a foregone conclusion that I, being the lazy type, chose the railroad. Before leaving I went to see my highly intelligent and rebellious Aunt Anna, so she shouldn't get herself needlessly in trouble. On her table I found Otto Strasser's *Sayings of Hitler* opened to its most damaging page, upon which this bitterest of Hitler's enemies quotes him to prove his raving madness.

Gently I suggested, "Better hide this book until we have driven those intruders out. If one of them should come stupidly around here and find…"

She heatedly interrupted, "If any of his henchmen comes snooping, what he shall find is this book open on its most compromising page!"

Then she stuffed my rucksack full of chocolate, "You take care of them, Bryn! I know you will."

The railroad was jammed. So many lazy Norwegians! The Germans had been told the Norwegians always traveled to the mountains for skiing at this time of year, so they were not too suspicious. Or perhaps they were glad to get rid of strong young men in the capital. We were nearing Eidsvold and the German Front when an old conductor walked through the train and announced in the most casual voice, "There will be a military inspection in a moment."

We collected our rucksacks. As if by an ingenious conspiracy, the train slowed down. We jumped. I landed in a snowbank, rolled gently down the hill and laid buried in snow as searchlight beams swept the area. When the lights dimmed, I rushed into the forest. When the night became alive with gutteral voices and crackling boots I hid under a felled spruce tree, and cocked my six-shooter. A child's face, drowning in a huge helmet, was suddenly above me, peering down. A flashlight blinded me. None of us spoke. He turned the flashlight away and I could see his lips quiver. He cut his flashlight and scrambled off.

"Abt du was gesehen Fritz?" His comrades in arms must have been studying his trembling face.

"Nein, nien!" howled Fritz.

I walked all night and in the morning gingerly entered a farmhouse. A man's piercing glance intercepted me. I offered him some money and asked for meal.

"Where you headed?" he barked at me.

"Where you wish me to be headed?" I replied cautiously.

"Talking in riddles, aren't we!"

"Sometimes that's all you can do."

"You a Norwegian?" The question was suggestive of his stand and I ventured to bank on it, "On my way to the Norwegian Front, yes."

"Why didn't you say so? My house is yours."

Through the farmers' grapevine I gradually worked my way to the secret frontline of the Norwegian forces and took part in the battle of Elverum, a phantom skirmish to present students of history though future scholars may call it a crucial event that made it possible to continue and eventually win a war that seemed hopelessly lost at that time. If a handful of Norwegian farmers had been defeated instead of successful in that skirmish, Hitler might today have ruled the world, they might say. And how could that be?

The crucial theater of war at that time was the Atlantic. Hitler was winning there. If this victory became final, Hitler would have been so firmly established in Europe no American effort could unseat him.

The weight that tipped the scale in the battle of the Atlantic was the Norwegian shipping fleet, the third largest in the world. For this shipping fleet to rally to the Allied cause, a legal Norwegian government outside the group of the Nazis was essential, a Norwegian government who could order the ships, all around the world, to proceed to the battle of the Atlantic, where destruction awaited them, where sailors would be cruelly tortured and killed.

Churchill called the Norwegian shipping fleet worth millions of soldiers to the Allied cause. This shipping fleet was the prize package the Nazis hoped to catch through their costly thrust into Norway, so carefully prepared, so cluttered with ruses and tricks. Many of their warships hoisted French flags as they approached the coastal batteries, hoping to pass as friends. Some did, others did not, for there were Norwegians who had made a study of foreign warships and caused some of the mightiest German ships to be sunk by coastal guns; among them the large cruiser carrying the German High Command and Gestapo bigwigs up the Oslo Fjord. This is why the Norwegian King and government managed to escape from Oslo. A German agent, who had stayed and spied in Oslo for sometime under the guise of a salesman of lady's underwear, took over command, being actually a senior officer, when the appointed commander was burned to a crisp in the Oslo Fjord. The new commander, General Falkenhorst, was severely scolded along with all major actors in the operation, for having let the Norwegian King slip through their net. The German air attache was then ordered to take a blitz unit north for capturing fugitives.

A handful of farmers who ambushed the air attache at Elverum made it possible for the King and government to move on and cross the border to Sweden. The Germans, in wanton revenge, bombed the village of Elverum to a pulp, killed people who did not know the word "German". It was about this bombing a Nazi bomber pilot boasted to me a few months later, "Every sortie and every bomb target is carefully planned by experts." And that in these matters he and I were "... too small fry to question such plans."

The progress of the Air Attache's blitz unit had been reported by grapevine. An adequate number of farmers with shotguns and bear guns gathered at a suitable thicket along the approach road.

As stuttering bursts of the German engines were heard in the distance, some of the farmers stopped chewing. The tobacco juice trickled down the cheek of one. He made no move to dry it off.

When the farmers could see the whites in the eyes of the German drivers, they still did not fire. But each one took aim so that every single German was covered. When each farmer could look straight at a car in the road in front of him, the one farthest ahead, aiming at the lead car in the convoy, nodded once. There was just one gun report, a twenty gun salute. Not one German remained in fighting form. Some were writhing in the mud, others were crumpled in their seats. Most of them screamed in agony. The farmers chewed a couple of times, then one said, "We can't leave them like this, t'ain't human!"

There was no first aid equipment around, no ambulances. All that had been destroyed or commandeered by the Germans. The farmers lifted their guns and continued shooting, until there was no more screaming.

Chapter 4

The Huldre

Was there ever an enchantress so ZAP? A witch so deliciously wicked? Her beautiful virgin features are belied by her furiously twirling cow's tail, reminding you that beneath the ethereal beauty there is a shameless passion!

When such a powerhouse descends upon a lonely ski man, lost on the mountain on moonlit nights, when she approaches dancing upon the icebound glades, stroking his chin with a slightly-perfumed hand, which makes her tail rise and twirl and whip around in a frenzy of passion, who can resist?

So he follows her, follows her right into her mountain cave where her father, Dovregubben, the mountain troll, puts a tail on the ski man too, so he will be one of the family and he is accepted and adopted as the Huldre's mate, one of many. To his human friends he is lost forever. To the Huldre's little brothers and sisters he is a new playmate, or a new victim, to be teased and bounced around on hooked spears.

Captain Redburn and I came to know her so well as she bounced out of thousand-year-old folklore to tease and please us with her stirring appeal, steeling us against a merciless invader whom, we were convinced, she resented and despised as much as we did. Redburn had been with us all the way from Hamar. He added graceful fun to our grim business. He was the best of the MI-5 and the ski expert of this playful outfit. His hitch with the Norwegians was clean, good hunting to this British champion—until one day at Mysuseter.

The events in which Captain Redfern played such a delightful part has been termed, collectively, the Battle of Gudbrandsdalen which followed the Battle of Elverum.

The screams of the dying were still ringing in our ears when the bombers came. First they dropped incendiaries which fell in a potato field, digging a neat ditch with a zigzaging purple flame. We watched, thrilled—did the Nazis just want to show us what they could do: the new warfare, the wave of the future, ditch-digging fireworks?

Then came the explosives. Light wooden houses were thrown in the air and came down, settling in ridiculous postures. Half a man stuck up from the debris of sand and rocks. The other half was buried. He was already beyond pain. Calmly he asked me to move his head over to one side so he could breathe a little easier.

Then we both saw the girl. She would have been about nine. Only her head was visible above the debris. She blinked, then tears streamed down her face. Obviously she could not speak. The tears ran out and her large eyes bore a thousand questions. Then as we looked, the light of her eyes went out.

I think it was this girl who cemented my determination. I resolved I would do nothing else until this sort of reasoning had been wiped out. People who believed they could achieve by such means had to be taught. Whether it would take five years or thousand years did not matter. They had to be dealt with, defeated, educated. All this determination would not have mattered in the least to the course of the world except for the fact that a few million others made exactly the same sort of vow for the same kind of reason. This was what defeated the brazen Nazi effort.

I remembered, at that moment, a show the German Embassy had put on for a select group of cabinet members and some congressmen in Oslo a few days before. It had been called a "Peace film". It was from Poland and showed the slaughter in the Warsaw ghettoes. It was in the interest of peace, said the promoters, because "it shows what happens when people refused to obey the command of a vastly stronger power."

But friends, what is strength?

While the Norwegian King and government moved east to Nybergsund and eventually crossed the border to Sweden, the headquarters of the Resistance moved to Hamar, southern port of the picturesque Gudbrandsdalen. In Hamar there was a steam bath.

This is where I met Captain Redburn. In the middle of a discussion about ski grease on the Ararat (the captain had just come from the MI-5 training center there) and as we were wallowing in the lusty froth of suds, the air raid siren wailed. The captain looked at me. My duty as host, I felt, was to make sure he was well-rinsed and was allowed to complete his bath in lazy comfort. With deliberate care we rinsed, dried, dressed. It isn't every day you can have a steam bath in war.

Just as we left, a bomb crashed through the roof. The walls flew out at us. The captain brushed his tunic. "Rude. They splattered us."

Captain Redburn had his revenge. The German troops advanced in a long drawn out column through the Gudbrandsdalen. The captain was attached as observer and strategic advisor to Norwegian ski troops harassing the German approach. "Harassing" proved to be the wrong word. In one single battle, 1700 Germans bit the dust while one Norwegian was lightly wounded.

"Well," the captain said, expressing the excuse civilized people require while slaughtering their fellowmen, "they asked for it, didn't they? They weren't invited, were they? They killed the little girls and boys whose fathers or mothers has never harmed him, didn't they? And they splattered us."

The Allied strategy, luring Germans into the narrow valleys and mowing them down from the hillsides, worked fine until that day at Mysuseter. This was a little mountain hamlet above Otta which the battered German troops had just reached.

We were gathered around the radio listing to Neville Chamberlain, "… we have found it necessary to evacuate Aandalsnes…"

Aandalsnes was the connecting point for all British and French troops in southern Norway. Evacuation of that port meant that the British had written off southern Norway. The Britishers still in this area were on their own.

Redburn's face paled, not from personal fear, I felt sure, but because of the decision to abandon a hard fighting ally just when success seemed so near. How near, even Captain Redburn did not know at that time. Months later, when I was a prisoner of the Nazis, Colonel Freising, Head of the German Military Intelligence in

Northern Europe, told me with the charming frankness reserved for hapless prisoners about to be shot, that the German High Command had been just on the verge of giving up the entire Norwegian venture and with going to Denmark, "in view of the murderous resistance of the Anglo-Franco-Norwegian forces."

That this bit of information eventually found its way to Allied quarters was due to the uncouth indiscretion of a prisoner who cheated death by running away from his firing squad.

Good old Neville Chamberlain, always so well-meaning, often so wrong! A few days' respite might have changed the course of the war.

Though he had reason to be timid. His predecessors, trying to ease the burden of the strange economy, has nearly stripped England of arms.

Captain Giertsen, head of the Norwegian ski patrol, told me to take Captain Redburn across the mountains to Sweden and be sure to keep out of Nazi traps for "Captain Redburn, if caught, would be tortured to death."

We set out that night while Nazi airmen slept and the snow was cold and bright so the skis ran along without human urging, a mystery revealed to initiates only.

On this night also, troll, goblins and elves emerged from hiding to dance, sing and howl along along the icebound glades. We could not see them however much we strained our eyes, but we could hear their voices blending with the muted music of streamlets beneath the ice—as I introduced them to the captain from the inexhaustible storehouse of Norse folklore. By and by he could hear them even better than I do. He had learned all that I could tell him during the long nights and added from his own keen perception.

Some of the troll wore British khaki uniforms and tramped determinedly through the snow, long columns marching eagerly North, others as hopefully heading West; others, again, South; some East, all with impeccable reasons for their particular direction. How glad they all were to meet the captain, how willing to listen to him and myself!

They all joined us, heading East, until we were hundreds, the captain and I ploughing a way through the snow on our skis, the others following at strategic distances in groups of six to eight.

Captain Redburn watched darkly when Nazi aircraft zoomed over us and apparently traced our tracks. Then he waited gloomily for the follow-up, the arrival of the ground forces. They never came. Why? He had the explanation: the troll! They were on our side! We had ample proof of this when, once, a plane alighted near our quarters and notified the Ground Forces who then came in imposing numbers on choice equipment up the road only to be stopped by a milling crowd of Norwegian farmers with hay forks and timber axes. They crowded the roads so no progress was possible for the armoured vehicles. They appeared deaf, oblivious to the Germans' urgings—until we were safely on our way, high up in the mountains. The troll!

It was my own confidence in the troll that made me walk down to that bridge where, Captain Redburn told me, peering through his glasses, German guns blinked in the sun and German uniforms were moving about. It was our only chance of a crossing and stubbornly I walked on alone, my British friends waiting behind trees on top of a hill. This seemed to me then the most tragic walk in my life. My mind was briskly walking in the opposite direction–nay, running! But my stubborn leg muscles would not obey. They walked numbly on toward what could be only cruel death or at least a lifelong hitch in a concentration camp.

But when I arrived, the magic of the troll had converted German bayonets into blinking Norwegian timber axes and the German uniforms to reassuring home-woven woodmen's garb. I waved my friends to come…

Then, on one moonless pitch-black night, as we sizzled down a steep slope dodging mighty pines, "Erik, the Huldre!"

I was as excited as the captain. Had we finally caught up with her? Should I at last be exposed to that legendary lure along with the splendid British champion?

The captain's voice was that of one thoroughly shaken, for while he had no doubt the Huldre was on our side, he did not trust his ability to resist her, and desertion, even into a mountain hideout of the fair Huldre, is not quite the thing for an officer of the MI-5!

But the captain's outburst was followed by a deep boom that, according to folklore, was several pitches below the Huldre's. "Nei, jeg er ikke noen huldre. Jeg er Olav Flaksjo. Vi har litt elgkjott aa by paa."

To Captain Redburn this speech made no more sense and was no more reassuring then if it had come from the real Huldre. He took a firm grip of my arm, as if to make sure the Huldre would not run off with him—or he with her.

The sturdy Norwegian mountaineer who had been waiting in the pitch-black night elected by the mountain grapevine, to welcome us with a snack of elk's meat, had understandably overshot in extending his hand to detain the captain and had hit the captain's chin—the Huldre's technique.

However, as our trip progressed I began to wonder whether Captain Redburn had not been right and Olav Flaksjo was not just another disguise the Huldre had chosen to adopt for our protection for she–he evinced an earthly foresight and premonition. That same memorable evening, in Olav's cozy log cabin, as Captain Redburn had gone outside for a moment to get his bearings from the blinking stars, Olav discreetly handed me a little piece of paper. "It will bring you luck," he said.

I looked at it. It was a crudely drawn American flag. I could readily see why he did not want the captain to know. British jealousy of the New World power and all that. But, however touching, I couldn't see what good it could do us. I put it in my pocket and forgot about it—until we came to that bridge across the Klara River. It was under repair, we had learned, and German soldiers would surely be there guarding it and keeping an eye on the repair. My English friends and I were discussing the situation briskly, while looking at a map and walking on.

The map must have been wrong, for suddenly a stentorian voice resounded in our ears, "Halte!"

We were already out on the bridge, facing twenty German soldiers under a fierce sergeant. "What are you doing here?" he roared.

It was then the Huldre put into my mind that I should pull out of my pocket the critically drawn American flag Olav Flaksjo had presented to me. Without a word I handed it to the German.

The sergeant fingered the drawing, looked at it with growing fury, then exploded: "You want to tell me the Americans will be here and fight for you…"

I had had no such intention, but it appeared to me the fury of the sergeant and his exclusive preoccupation with me and my American flag provided a fine opportunity for the English to get away. So I made frantic signs with my hands behind my back.

The sergeant promptly circled around me to look at my finger activity. "St. Vitus dance or something?"

Then only did I realize my efforts have been unnecessary. The English had correctly evaluated the situation long before me and had vamoosed already. The sergeant returned to the argument where he had left it.

"But I tell you, the Americans won't be in this at all. The Fuehrer has seen to that. Now scram, you dirty, ignorant Norwegian peasant, get going, I say; get out of here! Before I…"

"But sir, I only showed you a little drawing of an American flag, I…"

Then, abruptly, I realized the welcome meaning of the sergeant's fierce vocabulary. "Get out of here," he had bellowed and with relish I obeyed.

As I walked downstream, along the water, looking for a place to cross, I ached for my British friends who had disappeared without leaving a trace. No doubt they would get lost and be captured because of my negligence.

But here is clear, again, the Huldre came to our aid, for when I finally found a suitable crossing: a succession of slippery rocks, she caused me to slip on a midstream boulder. My skis careened, I stumbled and splashed into the roaring stream and was carried on at a sizzling speed until at last my feet hit on a rock and I could scramble to the other shore.

Bruised, shaken, and dripping wet I hauled myself onto dry land. There, at a place I had had no personal intention of visiting, were my British friends, huddled under a mighty pine. Captain Redburn came forward with not a trace of a smile upon his grateful face,

"This, sir, is what you call a sense of orientation. How in the world did you manage to find us?"

Upon the trunk of the pine under which we had gathered three crowns were carved—the Swedish border.

Then, as if summoned by radar, two uniformed guardians of Swedish law came stomping along on ashen skis with dignified, old world bamboo bindings. Their sober faces expressed no gleeful wish to embarrass but rather a studious wonderment about how they could twist the law to our advantage.

We had made up the story to match their hopes. The three Britishers in my immediate company were converted to salesmen of fishing tackle in Norway, when the war had suddenly overtaken them. The rest of the Britishers, who would arrive later, would have to make up their own yarns. So, at the police station, I gave a stirring account of these peaceful salesmen having been caught between the jaws of a cruel war. To prove my contention I offered eagerly to empty Captain Redburn's rucksack on the table, a sack specifically prepared for such demonstration.

The first item to come bouncing out was a formidable British army handgun. It clunked insolently against the policemen's cozy iron stove and then went off with an earsplitting explosion.

The two policemen thoughtfully stroked their chins, appearing to have neither heard nor seen. I was advised I was free to leave, as a Norwegian. The Englishman would have to stay. I urgently requested to stay and explain their plight. The policemen shook their heads: for the safety of all concerned, please, no further explanation from my side!

Imagine my relief when, the very next day, my British friends joined me in Stockholm. Together we proceeded to the cocktail jungle, Captain Redburn hailed as the king of raconteurs, as he portrayed, stars in his eyes, the incomparable Huldre, with a face like a virgin, who had caressed his chin and whisked him into the mountain, passionately twirling her telling tail, while he was treated to the side-splitting performance of the court troll bouncing captured Gestapo agents about at the points of their spears in a ghoulish game of hockey.

Chapter 5

The Phantom Sub

"Did you carry arms against the German forces?" This was the opening shot and an oral battle lasting well over three months, fought in Nazi-occupied Norway in the latter part of 1940 and involving a phantom sub, a genuine Navy Goat, stale German beer and a few Gestapo dignitaries who had tortured Norwegian patriots both before and after what they didn't do to me. Unharmed, I slipped through their claws to Allied territory with secrets weighing heavily on my inexperienced mind.

Should I be ashamed? I certainly can take no credit for my unexpected success. I can only laugh now, recalling my thoughtless, stupid answers to their queries. By all rules of the game I should have been placed before a firing squad. Childish idealism even in some Gestapo brains, left me alive, and perhaps also the fact that I was not burdened with American army rules for prisoners, which say that, when captured, give only in your name, rank and serial number. Such stubborn reticence may well end in disaster and with no game shown for it.

When a soldier becomes a prisoner his status has changed entirely. He is at the mercy of his captors. If he still has the wish and the courage to continue the fight in his own way, he must certainly not show it. He has become, at best, an undercover agent. He must display moderate friendliness, moderate talkativeness, to an enemy who feels as sure of his own nation's right as the prisoner feels about his. Most prisoners know and feel this instinctively. They have a whale of a difficult time because the book is written by and bears all marks of inexperience.

If there is to be a book of rules at all it might run like this: "Keep your captors in suspense. Make them feel you have more to say and will say it. Then they will not harm you for fear they may miss the boat. Surprise your captors. Say the unexpected. Say only what is true and, of course, insignificant; it takes a thousand lives to cover one single lie and the sheer weight of this work dampen your spirit. Talk—by all means talk—about your grandmother's love stories, if you will, and never seem stubborn or even unfriendly."

The fact that I was exposed to a succession of lucky incidents has not brought on any delusions of grandeur or claim that this humble tale could save anyone in another war, a coming war, under other circumstances. This story is just a humble illustration of conclusions reached after seventy years of war or peace.

The handsome young captain who fired that first shot blushed deeply at the thought of such a heinous crime as carrying arms against his German forces as we faced each other across the table in the dining room of the good ship Pandia. This table, instead of its usual supply of solid ship's food, was now covered with books, papers and maps. The representative of the German army seemed to think he was perfectly justified in questioning, in a manner of a judge, a Norwegian citizen in a Norwegian port on a Finnish ship. Was this according to the rules of war, or was it rather one of the idiosyncrasies of the Hitler syndrome? My fingers itched to take on that man.

I was also thinking of the poster which we had found stuck on trees and telephone poles along our trek through the mountains a few weeks back:

"DEATH BY SHOOTING is the punishment for helping Englishmen, giving them food or civilian clothes, or showing them the way."

Did the captain in front of me know that, besides having carried arms against his German forces, I was guilty of every one of the crimes listed on that poster plus some more serious ones? Anyway, I couldn't be shot more than once. But the Nazis were experts at making people somewhat uncomfortable before they were shot. Would the number and severity of my crimes single me out for such honor? What preparation did I have for the ordeal to come? What degree? Should I concoct fancy tales? Too complicated and too much fuss spent on the unworthy. I magnanimously decided to answer slam bang bash into the questioner's face as the spirit moved me or teased me.

Karl Stenbom, a Swedish businessman and I were the only passengers. We had boarded the Pandia in Petsamo with tickets for America, which we were made to understand might mean England. Off Tromso, "the Paris of the North", rather than alluring Parisian siren songs came a rasping roar out of the Arctic fog. It was followed by a staccato drumming: machine gun bullets ricocheting from steel plates. A Nazi fighter plane became visible. Its signal lamp blinked furiously.

It took sometime for the Pandia's signal man to read him. When he did, Pandia made about-turn with such zest she nearly capsized. When we reached smooth water near Tromso, the pilot alighted, unfolded a rubber raft and came aboard. Blue eyes gleamed.

"Why didn't you respond to my signal?"

"We did eventually, kind sir!" I replied in my best German, my right hand mockingly at salute, "But the visibility was low, attention unfocused."

"I had my hand on the bomb bay stick. One single egg would have sufficed for this old junk!"

"To think of it! We might not have had this nice conversation!"

"Have you heard Der Fuehrer's latest offer to England? It was just on the radio. He is so kind, our great Fuehrer, so generous! He still gives England one last chance. But I, for one, would be deeply disappointed if I did not get a chance to bomb England."

"Your colleagues bombed undefended Norwegian cities, killed little boys and girls. Didn't they know what they were hitting?"

"Every house, indeed—every point to be bombed—is mapped out in advance!" He strutted with professional pride.

"Then who mapped out the targets over Elverum?"

"That, my friend, you and I are too small fry to discuss."

The pilot had left and this dashing young Army captain had come aboard with appropriate retinue, and established himself in the dining room.

To his question as to whether I had carried arms against the German forces, I replied, "It is rather for me to ask: did you carry arms against the Norwegian nation? Did you cross the Norwegian border?"

The captain turned purple. His veins stood out. "You, perhaps, consider us Germans barbarians?"

"The Germans I met in Kandangan, Istanbul, and Berlin did not appear to be barbarians."

"Ah, so you know Germany, and Germans!" The captain smiled happily as if my knowing Germany and Germans could not fail to make me a friend.

His attitude was reassuring. It meant that he, at least, knew nothing of my crimes. His routine question whether I had carried arms against the German forces meant nothing, I soon realized. The Germans rather respected the Norwegians who had fought them in open battle. On the other hand, to give a stinking old pair of pants to a Britisher was a crime punishable by death.

The captain rose and shook my hand, "You will see great things going on in your country today!" he beamed. "Good day sir and good luck!"

A bulging civilian with bushy brows had been circling around and eyeing me surreptitiously during this dialogue. He looked like a bull—a not-unfriendly bull. His voice boomed, "Now I will take him over."

To me he said with a sly wink, "We shall have a look at your luggage, young man. Take me to your cabin." He was an expansive man who found pleasure in chatting and making a little propaganda on the side in a harmless way.

"Well, young man," he said as we tramped the steel deck toward my cabin, "You have heard about the terrible Gestapo, I presume? Now, I am of the Gestapo, was one of Hitler's first men and I don't look so bad, do I?" He smiled shyly, convinced that he didn't look bad. I said something about concentration camps. "Just Communist propaganda!" he shrugged. Then he turned watery eyes on me: "To have looked, just once, into those eyes (Hitler's, he meant) reassures you for a lifetime." He seemed on the point of bursting into tears.

We entered my cabin and he saw my rucksack. He fingered it rapturously, "What a typical Norwegian outfit."

He asked me to put all the papers I carried on a little table. Reassured by now, I spread them out with a flourish—and suddenly froze. There, among them, was the one paper I thought I had safely hidden upon my person: a letter of thanks for my "very special services", signed by the British military attaché in Stockholm only a month before. The strapping lions of the British coat of arms were partly covered by other documents. I eyed the devastating piece of paper. Should I try to retrieve it? Or shove it under other papers to conceal the lions? Too late! The best course now was just to wait and see.

The jovial Gestapo agent shuffled the papers. He pounced with glee upon some German translations of my employment certificates. One had the impression he was greatly pleased to find something he could understand. Then he looked down at the letter from the British military attaché with obvious distaste. Finally he shoved the batch of papers over to me.

"Well," he said, "these scribblings in Norwegian I couldn't possibly be expected understand."

How keenly I realized at that moment that ignorance is bliss. His blessed ignorance of English had saved my life!

"Certainly not," I agreed. "Norwegian is such an insignificant language, spoken merely by 3 million people. Why should anyone bother to learn it?"

He patted my back condescendingly, "Don't worry," he said. "You'll get along."

As the pleasant Gestapo man left, several alternative plans battled in my mind. Should I try to run across the mountains to Sweden while there was still time? Or follow the ship on to Harstad and hope for a continued trip to the United States (or England, really!) after the German authorities had completed their investigation?

A guard of six Germans on the ship was not a definite block to flight but constituted an additional hazard that weighed my mind in favor of staying aboard.

The ship's engine warbled its rhythmic accompaniment to the

chatter of a million arctic birds in the eerie polar summer as we moved from Tromso to Harstad.

Here three men of a different hue came aboard, two bald Navy captains and a young man with a high-pitched voice and a navy blue uniform adorned with silver instead of gold stripes. The three were know as the "Prize Commission" which, in war time, means a commission called to formulate the legal terms under which a foreign ship or "prize" should be looted and expropriated. The young man with the silver stripes, we learned, was a Gestapo lawyer.

The Finnish captain was questioned first, alone. He was a brave, honest, but short-tempered man. We could hear him shout angrily in there. He came rushing out, red of face, barking at me. "What's this all about?"

The sudden blast took me by surprise. I could only reply with a question. "What is what all about?"

"They asked all kinds of silly questions about you—wanted to make up my mind for me and tell them you came aboard from a British sub in mid-ocean."

"You know I didn't, don't you? So what are you worried about?"

"You a spy or something?"

"No, not yet. I'd like to become one someday to better help wipe out robbers and murderers."

The skipper grabbed my hand and squeezed, "Good boy! Those jokers had me' rudder knocked for a moment."

The first and second mate were questioned, as were the engineer, the firemen, the cook, the deckhands. All were asked the same question: which day, hour and where had they seen me picked up from a British sub?

When the other passenger besides myself, Mr. Stenbom, was questioned, we had surreptitiously opened the skylight and had a grandstand view, with perfect acoustics.

The little Gestapo man was studying a photo taken by the pilot who had machine-gunned the ship when Mr. Stenbom entered.

"This picture," said the Gestapo lawyer, "shows you standing on the poop while the ship was being machine-gunned. Why did you stand there? Weren't you afraid?"

"Afraid?" replied Stenbom, frowning resentfully, "Certainly not! Haven't you repeatedly assured us you came to protect us?"

The Gestapo representative sent him an ugly look but did not reply. He was hunting bigger game.

"Will you tell us," Mr. Stenbom, "Which date and which hour on that date was your Norwegian fellow-passenger picked up by this ship's boat from a British submarine?"

"I shall be glad to, sir. It was this morning at exactly 10:30."

"This morning? The ship was lying here in Harstad this morning. And at 10:30 the Prize Commission was already on board."

"Exactly, sir. While you were questioning the skipper, this British submarine appeared for the first and only time—in the first trial and imagination of a certain member of the Prize Commission. This is the only submarine we have ever heard of during our voyage."

The little Gestapo lawyer must have entertained thoughts of revenge, for he shuffled furiously through the Swede's papers, spread out before him, obviously in the hope of finding something incriminating. The Swede seemed equally determined to make him find something in that general category. He maneuvered a certain letter so that the Gestapo man couldn't fail to see it.

"What?" exploded the German finally, "You have a letter from Herr B…Ba…Bauman!"

"Yes," stated Mr. Stenbom matter of factly, "Bauman. The American who has offered one million dollars for Hitler alive, so he could put him in a cage as a showpiece."

"Do you… do you… share this Mr. Bauman's ambition?"

"Me? I should say not! I wouldn't offer a sous for the subject."

"Who introduced you to this…this…Bauman?"

"A friend."

"What was the name of that friend?"

"Mittler," said Stenbom in a barely audible voice.

"Hitler?" panted the Gestapo man, "You said Hitler?"

"I said Mittler," replied Stenbom as one who is thoroughly tired of being misquoted.

"Mittler? Mittler! How could anyone have such a name?"

With the exceptional talents of any true Swede, Stenbom

produced this well-rounded show knowing the official neutrality of his native country was worth more to the German then the temper or ambition of a frustrated minor Gestapo agent.

When I was finally admitted—the last on the list—I wondered if the performance of the others, particularly the Swede, had brightened or darkened my own prospects. The Gestapo production of a submarine having placed me aboard must have been deflated, but this, in its turn, would have angered and irritated the producers.

Chapter 6

A Veritable Navy Goat

The Gestapo agent sent me a spiteful glance. The Navy officers looked covertly amused. "When did you pass the border to Sweden?"

"May 14th."

"Did you pass alone?"

"Yes."

"Where there Englishmen with you?"

"I believe I just said I passed alone."

"Were you seen with Englishmen?"

"Passing the border?"

"Don't split hairs! You were seen with an Englishman in the Norwegian mountains! In Stockholm!"

"And now I am seen with Germans, in Norwegian ports?"

There was a smashing sound on the table. The Gestapo man had flung down on it a little red book. It was my passport. He pointed to a word flushed with a stamp across the page, "What is that?"

"It says *gratis*, I believe."

"Yes. Now why would the English give you a gratis visa?"

"Probably so I can escape from German bombing raids."

"There are no bombing raids now—the war is over! So why the gratis? The British give nothing gratis! This word simply means… (now the Gestapo agent came sliding around to me and put his face almost into mine) it means… you are a British agent!"

I laughed, though without merriment.

"Well, well, during the first World War, I was accused of being a German agent—and now you are ranking me upward to be a British spy, a member of the elegant Secret Service—can you beat it? Me, who looks so outstandingly stupid?"

"You don't look stupid at all, you look shrewd!" fumed the Gestapo man and though obviously the outburst was not meant as a compliment, I promptly made it out to be.

"You don't say! Then you really think I could be one? A spy, I mean. You have made me so happy, sir, for this has always been my ambition!"

"A sound ambition," said the Gestapo man dryly, "If working for the right people. If it turns out you were working for the wrong people—not so sound. In that case I feel sorry for you."

"Why sorry? Life is a game, a play, isn't it? Whether the players are English or German, what does it really matter?"

"We have ways of dealing with British agents…"

"You don't say? I should wish to know of your methods, test my reactions to them. Some people, you know, become like steel springs under inordinate pressure, such as torture, for example. Others melt like wax. I have never had a chance to gauge my own reactions."

The Gestapo man rose and put his face very close to mine, again. It was glistening with unholy lust.

"We have means of making any man grovel before us!"

It was too tempting. His face was so charmingly close. With a "Really?" I rammed my forehead smack into him. It might be my last chance to try his guts and I wouldn't have missed it for a fortune. He screamed. Then he became pale and silent. Now, I thought, he is going to jump over the table and land on my head, like the Old Man of the Sea. Why had I angered him? I had been acting without planning.

Instead of jumping across the table, he seized the huge protocol of the Prize Commission. When he hit me over the head with it? No, he just snapped it shut, banged it on the table.

"We shall have a talk with Oslo tonight. Tomorrow we meet again. You may find out that your funny business today has not helped you, has not helped you one bit. You acted so brave today like one who does not know fear. Perhaps we can teach you!"

The Commission left—after the guard had been increased to twelve.

While I was contemplating my next move without enthusiasm, a remarkable creature approached in a little native boat. Under a Navy cap was a wrinkled face framed in a goatee so rich and prominent I decided we were to be honored by the visit of a veritable Navy goat. He boarded the ladder with an alacrity that enhanced that impression.

The moment he set foot on deck he drew a formidable six shooter. Brandishing it, he lurched forward with such a hesitant gait I realized we had before us, not merely a Navy goat but a stoned one.

"Where is the captain?" he yelled, waving his weapon.

"I shall be pleased," I said, "to take you to him. Whom shall I say called?"

He stopped a moment and eyed me with an almost sober surprise.

"You—you speak German?"

I bowed deeply, "Sir, you flatter me!"

Enthused, he slapped my back and whacked my belly with his weapon,

"Ach, du braver Kerl! You not only speak German but you joke in German!"

This is how we exchanged pleasantries and entertained each other on the way to the Captain. I also was enlightened as to his identity. He was the German harbormaster.

At the site of the Captain's stockinged feet the German official resumed all of his ire. He pushed me out of the way and directed his weapon at the Captain's midriff. The captain stood his ground,

"Why did you stop this ship—a Finnish neutral ship going to a neutral country—America?"

"We Germans do what we damn well please for we have no friends in the whole wide world so we do what we damn please."

It occurred to me this uttering by the German official could be turned to my advantage, so I looked my goat friend warmly in the eye and declared:

"Don't say that! Don't say that Germany has no friends."

His decorative goatee trembled furiously as he endeavored to orient himself to my interposition,

"You— you, too, are talking against me now?"

"Certainly not. I am saying that although your lousy Nazi government may evoke little sympathy, the Great German People still have friends, will always have friends."

I saw the lovable face dissolve. Before he started to shed tears, I added hurriedly,

"Your genuine German seaman's soul will understand the Captain's plight. Here we have been kept aboard like prisoners without even a chance of going ashore and getting ourselves a smoke, a glass of beer, a tiny little beaker of schnapps. You will give us shore leave, I know."

The good German's eyes were blinking, the goatee was hopping up and down as he surveyed the entire crew that had gathered to watch.

"But, but—I could not possibly give shore leave to this entire crowd."

"Not necessary, good sir. Just to the Captain—and to me, of course. I will bring the stuff aboard."

So my goateed friend obligingly wrote out the shore leave, thus with the stroke of a pen undoing the insidious effort of the Gestapo man in increasing the guard from 6 to 12.

One more favor I demanded of my treasured friend: that he be my guide to shore. I smilingly shook my pocket filled with change, signifying there would be schnapps to boot. The Sergeant-of-the-Guard looked unbelievingly from my shore leave to his goateed compatriot who impatiently whacked him in the belly with his weapon yelling,

"Achtung! Aufrechts! Dummer Schweinehund!"

So, while the sergeant stood aufrechts, at salute, we boarded the harbormaster's dingy.

I left him in the Harstad Grand Hotel, mumbling unintelligibly to his goatee and took the main road toward the Swedish border leading also past General Fleiher's old residence, now used as German Army Headquarters. In my business-like briefcase were a toothbrush and a heavy sweater.

An entity blocked my way in the dark and hesitatingly lifted a rifle,

"Halte!"

My training in disposing of this kind of obstacle to progress had not yet taken place, so I stopped.

"Where are you going?"

"To German Army Headquarters."

"At this time of night?"

"Yes, and take me there at once! I am not disposed to idle talk."

At this salvo the German trotted along meekly to show me where German Army Headquarters were. When we arrived he had regained some of his erstwhile suspicion for he told the Colonel-Commandant,

"He was walking briskly along the main road to Sweden, sir. I thought it rather suspicious."

"You can go."

"Heil Hitler!" clicked the abashed guard, simultaneously with his tongue and heels.

I had my story ready, well-thought-out in advance.

"I am here on behalf of the skipper of the Finnish steamer Pandia. He wishes to send a wire to the owner. The skipper would have come himself but he doesn't speak German too well."

The Colonel and his aide, Oberleutnant Estra, found the request for reasonable and seemed inclined to comply. They went on to discuss the ship's cargo which was cellulose. Why would the United States import cellulose from Finland? It produced enough itself. Besides, there was Canada. The actual address was probably England.

I could inform them that Finnish export of cellulose to the United States has been going on for many years and to provide a little sauce which would make my argument tasty to the Germans, I added: "Cellulose, you know, is the raw material from which paper is made. Now what would England want with paper? Since the English, generally, neither read nor write? Even their toilet facilities are not overly sophisticated."

The Commandant shook from covert mirth and the Aide-Lieutenant guffawed openly.

This, I concluded, was the time for introducing my little personal problem:

"Nevertheless, your Gestapo brains, who seem to add no glory to the German image, are trying their darndest to make me out an enemy—me, with so many dear German friends!"

"Which German friends do you have?" The Commandant cautiously inquired.

"Well, Admiral Hans Schultze, my father's friend, who often came to our house…"

The Germans face darkened. Obviously there was something wrong with Admiral Schultze. Just my luck to post the higher ranks and flunk! Quickly I added,

"But above all, Freiherr von Bundschu, my colleague and friend who worked with us in Borneo."

The Commandant's face lit up,

"Ach! Freinherr von Bundschu! He's here, now, in Norway, a major on an—ahem—special mission."

So Bundschu it was. My Borneo safari may have saved my life.

He put in arm around my shoulder,

"My friend, are you being persecuted by the Gestapo?"

"Persecution is perhaps a strong word, but…"

"As a Norwegian soldier who rightly fought us as long as hostilities lasted," proclaimed the Commandant, "You are entitled to protection by the German army. We shall give you an escort back to the ship so you won't fall into the hands of those people. The request of the Finnish captain to send a wire to his owner is granted."

It was late when I came aboard. I spent the rest of the night pondering my prospects. By morning I had decided my best bet was to get away before my next scheduled encounter with the Gestapo, notwithstanding the ambiguous promise of the Army Commandant.

Dressed in a bathing suit, I appeared on deck shouting to the guards, "First man in!"

With that, I dived. This was to be reconnoitering, to see how they took it; a softening-up, to accustom them to see me diving.

I surfaced, waving, smiling,

"Why you sissies, you mama's boys, you water-scared greenhorns, why don't you come on in?"

They grinned sheepishly. One waved his gun hesitatingly in my direction as if in doubt whether I was game or tame. The Sergeant watched me furiously, red in the face.

"Come on up. Come on up, you!"

"Why?" I grinned, "If you want to talk to me why don't you come down here? Afraid of the cold? Mama's little boy?"

"It's against the rules!"

"Rules? I didn't know there were any. Now read them to me, from up there, and I'll tell you if they are any good."

The Sergeant actually produced a little booklet and began opening it. Then he thought better of it, smacked it shut and fumed, "Oh, you!"

This was enough for now. I climbed the rope ladder and thought I would make the dash late in the evening.

As I was shaking the water in my hair on to the Sergeant and kidding him, a boat came alongside. It was the Prize Commission.

The routine was the same as the day before. First the skipper, then the officers, then the crew, then passenger Stenbom, then me.

"Oslo informs us you are a person of note. Now why didn't you tell us?" The Gestapo man shouted as if I had withheld information strategically vital to the Nazi cause.

"Gentlemen," I uttered, "I am overwhelmed. First that someone in Oslo considers me a person of note; next, that this is supposed to be such a well-established fact that I should have known, and so informed you. Now, will you permit me to enjoy in silence, for a few minutes, the tremendous impact of this bit of news?"

"Why, you have written books."

"In Norway, everyone writes books. A sign of distinction would have been not to have written books. Even this modest requirement, I don't fulfill."

"The point is," yelled the Gestapo man, "if you had been just a peasant yokel, your meeting with some Britishers in the mountains might not have meant much, but when a man of distinction, who is not a mountain goat in everyday life, takes a three-hundred-mile trip to guide some highly-placed British officers to Sweden and safety, that becomes quite a story."

"Relax gentlemen. You are just overextending yourselves. I talked all this over quietly and in good taste with the Army Commandant of Harstad yesterday."

"The Army Commandant? Then you were ashore!"

"Sir," I said sternly to the Gestapo man, "where are your wits? How could I have talked to the Army Commandant without being ashore? So why the useless question?"

"Who gave you shore leave?"

"I should not dream of telling you. The way some of you Germans treat other Germans, you do not deserve frankness."

The Gestapo man jumped up like a giant out of a box. His face was white, his lips pressed together. This time he would surely have hit me, had not two Navy officers taken hold of his sleeves and gently pulled him down.

He smacked the big protocol shut just like the day before—no originality at all. Where was the reputed Nazi inventiveness, the "wave of the future?"

"We shall be seeing you," he said, though there seemed to be no enthusiasm at this prospect.

Should I have trusted the German Army against the Gestapo? I was not yet sure. I undressed and put on my trunks. This was to be the real thing.

Chapter 7

Stale Beer

There was a knock on my cabin door, "Some Germans here see you."

Three men introduced themselves as members of the Gestapo. I was wanted ashore. My elaborate preparations for flight by swimming has been wasted.

I dressed leisurely and followed my visitors. On the way to shore I watched the rich red rays of the arctic evening sun playing upon the fields and mountains. The impression was breathtaking. It was as if the scenery offered me its essence, its secret, its peak of beauty since this would be, I was sure, my last glimpse.

Then I faced my judges.

Again the little Gestapo man from the ship threw a little red booklet on the table in front of me. Again it was my passport.

"You are free!" He yelled as if utterly upset at the lack of justice in this world. I pondered his words, not yet able completely to comprehend, far less answer.

"When will you leave?"

I could not answer that one either. Nor could I see what concern of his this was, if I were really free.

"With the ship going south this evening at 8 o'clock?"

"All right," I breathed, reaching for the passport. The Gestapo man beat me to it, "We'll keep this a while," he growled.

Stenbom and I went to the cinema that afternoon. The picture was funny and someone sitting a few rows ahead of us howled with glee. When the lights went on for the intermission, he turned his head. It was our little Gestapo friend! As he noticed me, all merriment went out of him. There was no sound from him during the rest of the show.

Outside, we ran into Lieutenant Estra. Assuming he and his Colonel-Commandante and Major Freiherr von Bundschu were jointly responsible for my release, I stopped and thanked him.

"From now on," said the lieutenant, "you will meet other kinds of people."

He gave me an address: Oberleutnant Khul, Abwehr, Halden gate 3, Trondheim.

At the foot of the gangplank that evening, a Norwegian police officer edged over to me asking to see my travel reservation. His head came very close to mine.

"Don't look up now," he mumbled, "but you'll find a fat man with curly hair standing near the funnel. He is the German detective who'll be watching you."

During the long track south to Trondheim, the express steamer always calls at a number of ports, all of them pretty close to Sweden. Before deciding whether to try a dash for it or go on to Trondheim and see Oberleutnant Khul, I should size up my German shadow. Soon after we had left Harstad I accosted him and subjected him to intensive instruction in Norse folklore. For example, Hestmannen, the mountain he could see now just out yonder, had been pursuing the wondrous maiden Leikarmoen, just an ethereal shadow still further out. But Leikarmoen had other suitors so there was gun play and a neat hole was shot through Hestmannen —"Do you see the hole out there?"

The man yawned and nodded slightly, then excused himself, "I slept so badly last night. I'd like to turn in…"

He went down the stairs with a tired gait.

A few minutes later we called at Narvik. I looked behind the funnel. There stood my German friend, very much awake and watching the gangplank intently.

"Couldn't sleep, eh? Well, I know how you feel. I had an aunt once who also suffered from insomnia. I will tell you what, sir, read Norse folklore! That should put you to sleep. Do you have them in German? Never mind, I will tell you…"

I went on and on. Since he had cheated me and try to spy on me he deserved to be tortured in a mild way. But soon he yawned again and begged to be excused.

He always came up again, watching the gangplank. After I had ascertained this for five stops, I concluded it was an inveterate habit and bade him good night, went to sleep, happy in the conviction he would stay up all night and suffer because of me.

Next day I did not see him at all and speculated whether he had gone ashore or—happy thought—died from exhaustion. In Trondheim I mulled over in my mind whether I should try a dash for Sweden or go see Oberleutnant Khul. The name intrigued me—it means cool—so I went to Halden gaten 3. I read "abwehr-nebenstelle Trondheim" and rang a bell. A striking blonde in a nylon apron opened. Behind her was the kitchen with luscious-smelling pots on a stove. This looked promising. Someone behind me muttered, "No, it is the other door." It was my German detective from the boat.

Oberleutnant Khul had no chin but his watery eyes looked more authoritative to make up for the lack. For two whole minutes he just stared at me as if to fix in his mind the features of such an important object. Then he grabbed the phone.

"He is here!"

Then a raspy voice through the receiver: "Should we try some special persuasion on him? Give him a taste of the *peitsch*?"

The Oberleutnant looked testingly at my face, noted its mounting fury, its rapidly changing colour to pink, to scarlet, to purple. Possibly at this point, he remembered Major Freidherr von Bundschu.

"No, no, no, no, NO!"

This exchange of pleasantries about my educational possibilities was broken by a welcome entry: Mr. Stenbom, bristling with reserved dignity.

Oberleutnant Khul, now smiling as softly as if he had never heard that rasping suggestion over the phone, produced our respective passports, handed them over to each one of us with a magnificent bow, wishing to express the antithesis to uncouth Gestapo voices over the phone.

As we passed out of the door, Mr. Stenbom first, with me

trailing behind, the suave Secret Service lieutenant reached out a discrete hand and detained me while I was still half-hidden in the dark passageway.

"Would you come to the Hotel Muller tonight? We might have a bite to eat!"

So for me the episode was not over. The gentleness of the invitation along with my curiosity bade me accept. I weighed the prospects that I was going to be bumped off in a polite manner.

At the Hotel Muller the Oberleutnant introduced me to an almost Anglo-Saxonately dressed gentleman, striped trousers, morning jacket, and of course a shining monacle fastened by a black silk band.

"May I introduce Colonel Freising!"

Later I learned Colonel Freising was the chief of German Army Intelligence and all of Northern Europe. How in the world did I rate such an honor?

"Where do we go? Fjellseter?" This from the suave Colonel.

While the colonel's smart little DKW wound its way to the fashionable resort, Trondheim pedestrians looked hatefully at the German car and the brazen Norwegian, obviously enjoying the invader's hospitality.

At the Fjellseter a tremendous arrangement of tables in the form of a huge horseshoe welcomed to us. Ample vessels overflowed with lobster and shapely wine bottles radiated around us. How could all this be for us and at such short notice?

My host's face lit up at the sight but humbly he placed the three of us at an inconspicuous side table. With a glance at the bottles on the big table, he called the waiter.

"Bring some good white wine, please."

"Sorry, sir," said the Norwegian servant stiffly, "all our wine this evening is reserved for the City Council."

"Hmm. Let us have some lobster then."

"Sorry, sir. All our lobster is reserved for the City Council."

The colonel looked up at the waiter, "Is there anything you have that is not reserved for the City Council?"

"Oh, yes, sir; indeed, sir!" The guardian of the victuals smiled happily. "We have some German beer, sir!"

The slightly stale beer and day-old fish that was finally produced put the colonel in a contemplative mood, as if he doubted this fare would inspire in me the confessive zeal he had anticipated.

Nevertheless, he proceeded with the scheduled questions, such as, how high were the barrage balloons over Britain? How was the British morale now that, for the first time in history, they faced battle on their own soil? How did they eat?

I had been in Britain three months ago. Didn't he have any more recent sources? Nevertheless, I answered as if the fate of Germany and the world hung in the balance. The height of a barrage balloons seemed to be at least 200 feet, I said. Then I thought better of it and corrected this to 600 or perhaps even 1000 feet or more. Or perhaps I have been mistaken the other way and ought to think in terms of 50 feet. I spoke the whole truth and nothing but the truth. So ignorant was I of the real height that my guesswork was perfectly honest. The British morale, I said, seemed unshaken since the English apparently were too stupid—or too prescient—to realize they were to be battled on their own soil.

Then, suddenly, "With which ship did you come from America?"

This was an awkward question for if the colonel did not already know, he could use my information to squeeze the Norwegian ship owner because his ships worked for the enemy. To that, again, there was the answer that all available ships had temporarily been taken over by the Norwegian government in London and the owners have had no say over them any longer. So possibly there could be no harm in my telling. But I stalled by telling the colonel it would be embarrassing for me as a Norwegian to reveal the name of the ship until I had conferred with the owner.

"As you wish," he compromised gracefully; "however, it being so far back it can't hurt anybody now."

This, of course, was nonsense but I pretended to be impressed and to weigh the matter in the new light he had shed on it.

I received the blessings for my continued journey to Oslo and new addresses to be contacted there. Anticipating a new horde of detectives on my trail, I asked if my two new friends had any objection to my visiting the mountains on my way south. This meant I would be close to the Swedish border.

"But, my dear Sir," the Colonel's face expressed mild astonishment, "you are in your own country, aren't you? Why ask us?"

I gave them a brief and, I thought, spirited account of the guardian angel assigned to me on my trip from Harstad and suggested if there were to be a new angel he might be informed about my trip to the mountains.

The two officers bowed stiffly and remained silent and unimpressed by my performance.

Chapter 8

The Finn, A Cunning Man is He

Had a shadow been assigned to me on the trip from Trondheim, it must have been an accomplished shadow. I never saw it. In Oslo I rented a room in the house that had formerly been my father's and set out to pester the Germans. One of my rackets was that of an eager do-gooder. Every other day I had a new scheme for the Herrenvolk to consider. Once it was getting food through the Allied blockade—a creditable cause for a hungry Norwegian patriot. Closely related to this was a much later plan for making Norway a shining example of wealth and prosperity under benevolent German guidance.

A host of German officials listened politely, some even seriously. Others, like Herr Landsat Schmidt, tried rudeness which was a greater challenge. Landrat Schmidt was telephoning when I entered. With his back to me he bellowed into the receiver: "Ich lasse mir sows nicht zweimal sagen!"

Then he slammed down the receiver and roared into my face: "You come in regard to this food business. Well, in this matter you are not wanted! Not wanted! Understand?"

"No, sir. I don't quite understand!" I smiled sweetly into his angry face, "I don't understand whether it is me as a person who is not wanted, or me as a Norwegian, or simply me as anyone—anyone other than yourself."

My fine distinctions seems to require his full attention. He looked deeply thoughtful and his anger had vanished. Then he smiled. The solution was coming!

"I would say," he said mildly, "the more cooks the more waste. Do you know that old saying? You know what I mean, don't you?

Nothing personal at all! I should be glad to talk to you any time on anything else."

I promptly switched to the well-fed prosperity business, emphasized how he, as a German official in Norway, would wallow in delicacies. His fat face dissolved into pleasant dreaming.

It would be deserved, I added, considering how he and his German colleagues have taken their lives into their hands by coming to Norway whose fierce underground workers any day might slip a silk cord around his neck and tighten it! He grabbed his throat, a look of terror replacing the erstwhile smirk.

Under cover of such a gentle surface activity, I could safely work for the Norwegian underground. My constant contact with the Germans enabled me to accomplish small missions. One concerned a new airfield 30 miles north of Oslo. On a dark October night, Fire Chief Klaussen phoned me to meet him at the corner of Suhm Street and Kirkeveien at seven the next morning. In underground code this meant one block east and north and one hour earlier. So at six the next morning I waited at the proper corner until Klaussen's large Packard eased up to the curb. I hopped in and enjoyed his latest gossip. As Fire Chief, having studied at a German university, he enjoyed the confidence of the Herrenvolk.

As we reached the airfield, Klaussen circled it several times so I could take in the details of the terrain. Then we zoomed through the gate, which was held open for the Fire Chief and his "Assistant", the guards at salute. Klaussen called on the officers-in-charge of the various functions of the field and had them reel off information on schedules, capacity, construction, runway lengths, etc.

Then he frowned, "Where is the Commandant?"

"In his quarters, I believe – a – he was not very well this morning."

"Not very well, eh? Not well enough to receive me when I came here all the way from Oslo to inspect his work for the safety of his men and material? Well, please convey to him my sincere regards and wishes for his precious health, will you?"

Klaussen fussed around his car long enough for the abashed Commandante to appear.

"My apology, Mr. Fire Chief; Mr. Klaussen, sir, I really did not feel very well. Would you care to come to my quarters for a little refreshment?"

"No, thank you. I was of a mind to report your absence to your superiors in Oslo. Perhaps now I won't!"

Entering the car, he slammed the door shut and zoomed off.

When we were outside, I complimented him on the performance in general, but doubted the wisdom of his blast at the Commandante.

"That," he said, "was the most important of all. Now we shall have no detailed report from him to Oslo about this inspection and the Assistant sitting in the back of the car."

Maybe there was a report after all, or maybe the Germans drew their own conclusions from the fact that the airfield was bombed and destroyed almost beyond repair on the day following our visit, for that very same evening the underground informed me my goose was cooked, my usefulness exhausted and I should vamoose. Not too long after that, Gestapo agents were marching up and down before Klaussen's home with a picture of the Fire Chief in their hands. He saw them first and escaped to England.

Apart from the airfield adventure, Klaussen had also investigated the bodies of a group of Norwegian patriots who had died from torture and were to be cremated. He found they had been subjected to enemas with boiling water. This treatment adds fear of death to the pain and mostly makes the victim talk. The Nazi inventiveness in the field of torture had gone beyond that of the middle ages.

Just after the underground had warned me, I met Colonel Freising in Klingenberggaten in Oslo, outside the German Army Headquarters. I greeted him exuberantly while reading in his face the marked suspicion caused by the reports he had received. I slapped his back unnecessarily hard and insisted we go to Blom, the favourite hang out of all good Germans in Oslo. I saw to it that the Colonel had plenty to drink.

He became pleasantly talkative, he told me nostalgically about his time as a spy master-butler in a massive Long Island mansion belonging to an American financier where statesmen and business leaders discussed the hottest topics of international intrigue. He was found out, and bolted through a kitchen window, after which he lived with the Long Island ducks for a while.

With the facility of the inebriate of quick change of subject, he now switched to the first days of the Norwegian battle and how the German High Command had been on the verge of giving up Norway and returning to Denmark "in view of the murderous resistance of the Norwegian guerrillas"—but then, the British Norwegian high strategy of "saving men" while luring the Germans into the valleys had saved more Germans than freedom fighters.

He now turned to genuine prophecy:

"Germany will win many battles as in the last war, but is headed for ultimate smashing defeat because, as always, we have the world's best soldiers and most stupid politicians!"

At this point I casually breached the subject of a pass to Sweden.

"Isn't it a shame," said I, "how the German military efficiency that you have just now so eloquently portrayed, has deteriorated to such an extent that you can't even wrest from these slow moving bureaucrats a simple travelling visa."

He was aroused. "A shame!" he agreed, "I shall go with you in person. We will see if the old efficiency can't be evoked again."

I wondered, then, how a drunk security officer would fare in the German passport office. But I needn't have worried. It was past quitting time. He insisted we go first thing, next morning.

In my mind I wrote off the incident. How could I expect him to string along, when, in the morning, he would wake up sober?

I kept the appointment, however, and who could have been more surprised than I when I found him waiting, calm, sober, exquisitely attired?

He flashed a tiny shield before the German passport officials, they straightened up, hopped to his command, and in a minute I had my visa to Sweden.

Who can explain the intricate ways of intelligence? By all normal reasoning I should have been shot or at least detained. British Intelligence, duly weighing the case, concluded that if I were not, unknown to them, secretly serving the Germans (a double agent), another explanation might be that the Germans preferred to get rid of me rather than waste time on a thorough investigation, since they believed I had no further whopping secrets, and since obviously I was not a real friend. The Norwegian underground wizards added that Freising probably wished his German Army viewpoint about the Nazis to reach Allied Headquarters. Also Freising might wish to prepare for himself a niche in the world, after the Nazis should be defeated—by ingratiating himself with one of the Allied soldiers, however humble, at this early stage.

If Freising wished me well, others didn't or at least they didn't any longer when we neared the Swedish border. A team of German customs officers, who often were camouflaged Gestapo officers, came into my compartment. I now noticed that there apart from myself, was a young man disguised to look amazingly much like myself before I had been disguised.

"Where is the man going to in America?" they demanded to know. Before I had time to answer, my compatriot began stuttering, "Well, you see, I was only just going to visit an old aunt across the border."

"Across the border in America, eh?"

"Yes, yes, across the border in...no, what did you say? Across the border in Sweden, of course!"

I did not know at that time that my compartment mate was a planted agent and decided I should not let him suffer for my crimes. Flashing with awakening conscience, I opened my mouth to speak when a heavy suitcase came tumbling down upon me from the rack above, while a voice rasped in my ear, "Keep your mouth shut, you infernal idiot!"

Well, if that was the way he felt about it, I was certainly not going to save him. I kept my mouth shut while my helpless substitute was dragged off between two sturdy "customs officers."

Later I learned what had happened to him. The Gestapo armoured knights, when realizing their mistake, had simply let him go. After all, jail space is expensive and cannot be wasted on the unworthy. The elaborate curses which they had thrown in my direction were relayed to me later on—salve upon frayed nerves!

After reporting to proper authorities in Sweden I reached Finland. In Helsinki I read American magazine articles about this valiant little country's so-called "complete subjugation under Nazi rule", while this well-organized nation managed to keep me out of reach of the Nazis during my entire trip.

However, after I had installed myself in my cabin aboard the SS Mathilde Thorden in Petsamo, the German Consul made an appearance. A serious and unhappy man with a fat neck and pince-nez, he showed me a card with my name painted in bold letters.

"Are you this person?"

I bowed agreement. "Nice" people don't deny their identity.

"You will have to go ashore—sofort!"

His attitude was a bit too imperative. Generations of democratic forebears decided my reaction.

"Mr. Consul, do you know what you were talking about?"

"What! What are you saying?"

"That you better watch your step. My trip was arranged by Colonel Freisling. Of course, everybody knows who he is."

At the beginning of this last sentence the Consul was still on his high horse, but at the end of it, his voice had dropped down to a reverent whisper and his eyes watered uncertainly behind his pince-nez – Freising! The Intelligence Chief! The horrible fear of butting into a delicate mission gripped the dutiful German.

"I - I - I - We must wire Freising at once!"

"Easier said than done, Mr. Consul. Colonel Freising is at this instant on his way to Belgium."

Another low on the financial barometer of the German was registered. My knowing the travel schedule of the intelligence chief indicated even stronger to him that I was on a secret mission for the German forces. He shifted his weight from one foot to the other.

"We must wire Berlin," he decided. "The ship must wait."

Now the skipper came to my aid.

"Sailing permission has been given already. Each additional hour of waiting will cost $118.60. Before I can agree to let the ship wait I must be informed who is going to pay."

"The ship must wait!!"

The imperative tone was back, though more in the way of a howl than a command. The skipper eased himself into an armchair and produced a game of cards, "Care to join us, Consul?"

"No!!"

Then, as the skipper and I played, every quarter hour he looked pleasantly at his watch, "One quarter—$29.65, Half an hour—$59.30…"

When he had announced the two hour strike, and "$237.20…"

The Consul rose with a suddenness we had not expected in view of his girth and sobbed, "The ship can leave!"

Then he strutted ashore, his fat neck being our last view of the Nazi might.

In New York a letter arrived, a beautifully typewritten missive from the Helsinki office of the Finnish steamship company, readdressed from the hotel I had stayed in at Petsamo before embarkation. The letter stated,

"Dear sir, owing to circumstances beyond our control, we are sorry to inform you that it will not be possible for you to leave with our ship, the Mathilde Thorden."

So the reply from Berlin had arrived at last, and had been dutifully transmitted by a law-abiding steamship company, no doubt with a carbon copy for the German Consul.

Chapter 9

To Kidnap a Head of State

I was part of an international band assigned to kidnap Hitler. First we had just assigned ourselves. Following this, we were assisted and egged on by an ever-growing crowd of notables, including intelligence bosses, generals and statesmen until the supreme personality in the Allied leadership turned us down.

Wars tempt us to play along the surfaces, though in the centers sit dictators, the Hitlers and the Stalins, players whose pawns are soldiers who form cushions protecting the crimes and the criminals. Rather than fighting these innocents with our own innocent soldiers, airmen, swabs and spies, we crave to hit the center.

Our plot developed almost by itself. Hitler was so notoriously kidnap-able. No other person in history was such an obvious fraud and so reckless.

Stalin may have been comparable as a person, but he was much better protected and, despite his monstrous acts, he had more sincere followers all over the world. His secret police effectively hid the smouldering sentiments of his victimized subjects. Above all, we were never in a shooting war with Stalin's Russia.

With Hitler everything fell into place. We were in a hot war with him, or rather with his Nazi party. We had ample proof of widespread discontent in Germany. Half of Germany's men were eager to risk their lives in an effort to rid Germany of a nightmare.

The Nazi party's first serious challenge to Germany and the world came with a depression in the early '20s, which caused a quarter of the votes to be cast for the Nazis in 1924. During the boom of 1928 the Nazi vote sank to a fraction; then rose to 44% in 1933 when Germany shared with us "the Great Depression."

I lived in Germany at that time and watched how this crisis evoked memories of the early 20s when millions starved. This frantic mood upped the Nazi vote. Still, 44% is no majority. Through lies, blackmail and a few well-planned murders, Hitler sailed into power. Therefore it was not surprising that a strong anti-Hitler underground sprang up immediately. Among its leaders were Generals Beck and Hammerstein, top army men, later to be joined by Generals Rundstedt and Rommel, famous wartime army commanders. Among civilian members were Leipzig's Mayor, Lederer Conrad Adenauer and Willy Brandt, both later becoming Chancellors of West Germany. The approaches of this group to Allied statesmen and church leaders have been widely publicised. There was another side to the story that now may be revealed.

Having owned a business in Berlin, (Orientalistengemeinschaft) and even being able to pronounce this name, I was considered a linguist of note and a point of contact. My escapades in occupied Norway had further endeared me to British Intelligence.

In the summer of 1943 while Londoners slept in the subways with suitcases for pillows, occasionally surging to the surface to laugh derisively at the Germans raiders, Germans rank and form buck private to General arrived fresh from Hitler's Headquarters to MI-5. Colonel Malcolm Munthe of that body—tall, polished, patient listened for hours as they talked. In response, a plan of operations emerged which the sober minds of the merely fact finding MI-5 were not permitted to even dream of. Colonel Munthe called on a general of a bold operational unit. The general's worry wrinkles deepened appreciatively.

Our German guests had painted a picture of anguished confusion at Hitler's war headquarters. Irate generals would come bursting in, pleading for or demanding changes in important commands. Hitler fumed, a real hassle would develop, and often just because the generals had already made the changes and hoped Hitler would comply.

Our plan took off from there. We proposed to be the next such group of irate generals, elevated into the highest ranks by the matchless art of London tailors, aided or abetted by proper insignia and decorations. Instead of pleading for decisions already made, we would invite Hitler to come along with us to make his own arrangements. We would invade Hitler's sacred area, in aircraft properly marked and flashing the right signals. Landing, we would make our way "sofort" to the Feuhrer, preferably by exclusive use a weapons of wit, though if necessary aided by hardware.

From that point on, circumstance would be our guide and decide for us whether we could have the best, the next best or the third best. The best would be if Hitler could be persuaded, without hardware, to go along to our "headquarters" and make the "desired changes." He might go by his private plane or our plane. In any event, we would in due time have the course changed to England. The next best would be to have the same accomplished with a bit more substantial persuasion. The third best would if we should have to shoot our mustachioed friend, a course that might break our tender hearts but—well, yes, of course, there were even grimmer possibilities.

Any of the alternatives were likely to rid the world of Hitler, so the chances of survival of the mission members were slim indeed. This was our least worry. We, prospective participants, had entered this war to win, whether this took dying or not. And what satisfaction dying in a worthy and decisive endeavour! An earnest resolve was aglow in us as our plans matured and we were reinforced with countless but important details. No one could have been more serious than we as we envisioned our children and grandchildren answering when asked how daddy died: in fighting Hitler in person, rather than battling his cushion, the innocent little buck privates down to 18 years of age.

The general with the wrinkles, at least, was sufficiently impressed to take the plan to—would it not be preposterous for a mere agent and adventurer to boast where?

There were whispers about a British cabinet meeting, a secret session dominated by handsome Anthony, and thunderous accord. Then onward went the plan—said the whisperers—to higher stations across the ocean.

I watched the mighty V-I robots thunder over London like a

thousandfold motorbikes under flaming crosses. When silence struck and the bikes turned downward, I ran for shelter—something I had never done before. I would not miss my trip with Hitler! Also, I counted the days until these raids would be over—thanks to us.

Days trickled into weeks. These, in turn, strung into months. We spent the waiting time improving our plans, shopping around for adequate aircraft, painters, outfitters, experts on markings and signals. Everything was kept up to the minute. We filled in new details every day, tightened the structure, secured loose ends until we became scientifically convinced we must succeed, a sound condition for any mission though almost never realized.

We took comfort from the fact that while we, the mission members, were but a handful, our ideas were widely shared. Alan Dulles, later to become head of the US Central Intelligence Agency and Trevor Roper, noted British historian and intelligence officer, repeatedly advocated collaboration with the German underground for disposing of the Hitler regime. Of course the G.I.'s of all units, British tommies and little German teenagers with guns were already talking our language. And British General F. C. Fuller, who knew of our plan, took time out to write a series of the articles in the London Press intended to weaken two Allied dogmas we feared might stop us.

"We must defeat the Germans so they know they are beaten!" was one oft-repeated statement. General Fuller pointed out that the Germans we would cooperate with, representing at least 56% of the nation, needed no such prompting—and that the rest could not be taught, and did not matter.

"Unconditional surrender!" was another slogan. General Fuller wrote that any surrender implied conditions and that "unconditional surrender" was simply an anomaly.

We were proud and grateful to have a man of General Fuller's stature secretly, yet openly, rooting for us and that the British permitted him (and others) to write freely against officially accepted policies. We began to feel success in our bones.

Six months had gone when Colonel Munthe called me to his office. I looked at his face and was surprised it did not show signs of victory I had so surely expected. Word had come to the general with the wrinkles, who had told it to Colonel Munthe, who now told it to me:

"We won't play."

Again there were whispers. August personnel among the Allied had argued that on such a momentous decision Stalin must be called in. From that moment on people in the know lost faith. They knew he would never go along. Why would he consent to a plan that would end the war while his armies were still far from Berlin and other coveted points? Besides, continuous war would permit him to get rid of more undesirable Russians at the front or through purges fitting into a war hysteria. And he wouldn't mind a few more Americans and Englishmen killed either, in addition to his own undesirables!

A huge cross of fire roared outside the windows of the MI-5, then stopped and turned nose down, right toward our building. My whole world seem to me as certain of destruction as the target for that robot. I was ready for it.

A deafening explosion shook the building and long after shattered glass tinkled and rustled. Then I awoke as from a bad dream and collected my unbroken limbs and numbed mind for new battles.

Such was the tragic story, tragic for the millions of men, women and children of all participating nations who were killed and whose lives were worse than wasted because the plan to end the war at a time when it had served its purpose was rejected.

What about the future? Should we just plan to kidnap any head of state who is waging war on us?

No, the message of the story is simply that we should keep informed about any country we may go to war agains—informed about its temper, its nature, its leaders and their standing, character, stability—just as some of us were informed about the Germans and their Nazi leaders. On the basis of such up-to-the-minute information we will know what to do and whether a thrust against the center may be tried.

CHAPTER 10

THE LITTLEST THINGS

SABOTORGRUPPEN PAA RJUKAN
Reddet New York, Chicago og San Francisco
FRA TOTAL ODELEGGELSE

Saturday, September 29, 1945, the Norwegian paper, *Vaart Land* featured this headline in bold type on its first page. It means "the group of saboteurs to Rjukan saved New York, Chicago and San Francisco from total destruction."

I rushed through the sensational article and found, to my consternation, it was wired from San Francisco to Oslo as a result of my own talk the preceding Friday to the Commonwealth Club of California. They were not my words but a bold deduction made from them.

Rjukan is a wild and dashing mountain range in the south of Norway, with one of the world's great waterfalls, rock in Rjukan-Fossen, partly tamed to produce power for a huge fertilizer plant. There was power to spare which was used for various projects, among others the production of water in which the hydrogen atom had a neutron in addition to its proton. This made the hydrogen atom heavier than usual. The production of heavy water was under the direction of the inventor, Professor Tronstad, at the Engineering University in Trondheim. He commuted back-and-forth between Trondheim and Rjukan.

When the Germans invaded Norway they had first showed no interest in the Rjukan heavy water production. This was fortunate, for heavy water was considered one of the most promising moderators for an atomic pile and, what was still more important, a forerunner for a fusion process: in more familiar terms, a hydrogen bomb.

Then a professor at Oslo university, with Nazi leanings, became famous by swallowing a mouthful of heavy water, demonstrating that it had no toxic affect.

From this event, believe it or not, German interest appears to have been aroused. Against the gruff and angry protestations of Hitler and his half-educated personal staff, German scientists scrounged the necessary funds to start on the long track to develop an atomic pile with heavy water as moderator.

Naturally they sought Tronstad's advice. He kept them guessing while conferring secretly with London by radio. The inevitable happened. The German pressure reached a point where Tronstad had to flee. It came on so suddenly that he found himself running around in snow drifts and howling storms in the mountains in his pyjamas and slippers.

Tronstad was a healthy young man and eventually arrived in London no worse for the ordeal. I met him there early in 1943 busily planning how to frustrate the German effort.

So busy was Tronstad, so absorbed in his work, that he completely neglected the social life in London—the cocktail circuit. His British connections thought this was unfortunate since people might guess he was involved in some work connected with his colourful past. Such guesswork and a half-leaks that would follow must be avoided. So Tronsdad was advised to show up at a cocktail party. There a well-known female gossip took him under her wing.

"Oh, I understand, Captain Tronstad, that you are working on a very, very big thing?"

Tronstad, thinking of the tiny atoms and atom components of his daily work, replied innocently,

"On the contrary, Madame, I am working on the littlest things!"

The Secret Service blanched. What an indiscretion. Would the lady guess? Would the whole party know? Later again the world?

The lady put all at ease with her reaction, "Oh, now, Professor, I'm sure you're just too, too modest."

Tronstad was never again requested to attend the cocktail circuit.

Fresh reports from Norway in Germany hinted that the Rjukan

project was even more alarming that at first thought. German scientists, though unsupported by the Hitler crowd, had been moving fast. Their current plans called for high gear production of heavy water at Rjukan, then exporting it to the Kaiser Willhelm Institute in Germany. At this institute an atomic pile was already in the making. Heavy water production must be stopped at all cost.

Tronstad wanted to go into the grounds with a select group of saboteurs. The British proposed a glider raid. The Americans opted for bombing. Tronstad held this would be useless. The bombers would only destroy the upper stories of the plant, not the basement where the heavy water equipment was located.

First the bombers went in and alerted the Germans who doubled the guard and built electrically-charged fences around the area. The bombs destroyed only the upper floors and left the critical facilities in the basement untouched.

Then two gliders were launched. One fell into the ocean. All hands drowned. The plane pulling the other glider crashed into a mountain. The glider landed, violently. The survivors were taken prisoners though not treated according to the Geneva Convention. Eventually all were shot.

Tronstad had worked on his own plans while the bombers and gliders tried their luck. Now he had nine Norwegian boys ready except that two of ten boys were fighting valiantly to be the ninth. One of these latter was myself. Tronstad was agreeable but the British insisted all hands must be under 35. Tronstad countered that it had been seen that many people improve in alertness and resourcefulness after 35; then there was the added experience. A drawn out discussion and serious delay was not called for at this juncture so I tactfully withdrew. Little did the British know how I was to strike back at them.

The nine under 35s were dropped on the Hardinger Glacier, at a very safe distance from the plant. A single scout surveyed the approaches, then all worked their way toward the gates. In an early night they blasted gates and crawled through conduit tunnels. Various groups took up cover positions and two men entered the room with the critical equipment. Resourcefulness, courage and a good bit of luck had been required—so much that when I heard the boys talk about it I am not sure I would've liked it, for Tronstad's original plan that had looked so smooth could not be followed and the boys had to improvise. The plan called for descending from the mountains through a water tunnel that at this time carried no water. But the tunnel entrance was found inaccessible. The smooth easy way had to be abandoned.

The two blasters found only one man in the critical room, a single rather peaceful Norwegian guard, who let himself be tapped gently on the head. Unconscious and unblameable (from a Nazi point of view) he was hauled out of the room by the boys before the blast went off.

Some workers on the upper floors sensed that all was not quite regular down below. One reported,

"None of us felt quite happy sitting there waiting for whatchamacallit. It was as if waiting for the little earthquake we all expected to happen. When it did happen, it wasn't a quake, just a polite jolt. But when we went down to look, there wasn't a bit left of all that significant equipment.

The men from London had long since disappeared by then, out through those same tunnels and gates. Back in their mountains they started skiing on the long track through all of southern Norway into Sweden from where they flew back to London—all but three who remained to lead later saboteurs.

The event called General Falkenhorst, Commander of German Forces in Norway, to Rjukan along with Mr. Terboven, the civilian governor. When they surveyed the damage, Terboven swore. He was no gentleman. But the General said, "The neatest piece of work I have ever laid eyes on!"

This mission, of course, was only the first. Again and again Tronstad's men struck, different men each time. Twice the Germans had happily loaded sizeable amounts of heavy water in ships. One ship was destroyed by saboteurs, the other by bombers. There is a time and place for everything.

Tronstad, the planner, kept the world safe from German heavy water atomic piles until the war was breathing its last, and victory was seen. Then, as peace loomed and heroism and adventure would be hard to come by, he panicked, like so many other excellent leaders. He wanted to test his brute, physical courage and stamina. His pyjamas flight in the Norwegian mountains had not been enough. He wanted to show that he could do whatever he had ordered his men to do. Perhaps he was still haunted by that British objection to men over 35. So, on the last trip to enemy territory, a trip no longer strictly necessary, he hired himself as one of the members of the team. He did well and was about to start the trek back to England when a half-wit with a gun, a Norwegian quisling, happened upon the camp of the saboteurs and killed Tronstad with a single "lucky" shot.

Had Professor Tronstad really saved New York, Chicago and San Francisco from total destruction, as I had so boldly claimed that Friday in September, 1945, to the Commonwealth Club of California?

The hard truth is that probably he had not. His untimely death was even more useless than at first apparent. For it later became clear that heavy water was not such a good moderator for an atomic pile as first assumed. Apart from that, the entire German effort was on too small a scale to promise success in the limited time left to the Germans.

At present it looks as if the Allies would've been better advised to leave the Germans to stumble along unhindered with the heavy water moderated atomic pile and thus wasting scientific man-power, time and money on this inauspicious effort, to the comfort and aid of the Allies.

The Great Architect of developments, of human efforts in war and peace, would he not have wept and also laughed, looking at the gaunt heroics displayed, and the irreparable losses suffered in the pursuit of useless goals?

Chapter 11

Over the Hill into the Fire

Insubordination, to be successful and enjoyable, requires planning and dexterity of mind. Above all one must have a generous and powerful backer.

When the Normandy invasion beckoned to would-be heroes, I was a chairborne Captain in the Army, commanded by the Navy. Mailmen and messenger boys passed me by. Had the inscrutable wisdom of authority decreed for me to live out the war behind my desk?

The almost unforgivable indiscretion of applying directly to the War Office for a job at the Front became my only alternative. At discreetly-spaced intervals I ran up the stairs of that office, three steps at a bound, to underscore my adequate physique, telling whomever would listen about my languages and other pertinent or impertinent qualifications.

The mailman brought the inevitable answer to my desk.

For the last time, I ran up those office stairs seeking the author of the note of denial. The Colonel whose signature emblazoned this document looked me over coldly, wielding his monocle:

"We turned you down because you have been running the stairs of the War Office a bit too often. We don't like people who are too keen. And...the front is no playground! "

This last statement seem to me sufficiently interesting to be shared. I thought particularly of a young upstart in the world of the Britons—a youth who had done a bit of playing over the "playgrounds"—the Royal Air Force! The appropriate authority of that evasive body did not laugh what he heard my story. His eyes were hard, like steel.

"Will you come with us?" he asked simply, "We could use you —right away."

According to instructions, I appeared next morning in the uniform of an A–2, Air Force hand, at the assigned airbase. At that same hour my old Navy Commander found on my desk a discarded Captain's uniform with a note attached.

After a few days' instruction in how to behave in the wild jungles of France, the Warrant Officer sent us off with these immortal words: "Now dinna come and sye I dinna warn ya!"

Being in the Air Force now, I boarded my first Navy ship, naturally. Midway across the channel we were marched in single file past a hatch from which came a whiskey tenor: "You want it straight or in yer tea, matey?"

"Do I want what straight or in my tea, sir?"

"Yer rum, matey!"

That rum brought me safely through the ordeal of the landing. Additional swigs were required for surviving the lugging of petrol drums, loading of trucks, prodded by a sergeant who swore he would make an airman of me in spite of all!

Then the papers from London came through. I was summoned to my Commanding Officer, a Group Captain, now an Air Marshall. He told me to put on a Captain's uniform again, Air Force Captain this time, and continued: his most serious problem was recovering fighter pilots who had crashed inside enemy territory. Another 'must' was getting supplies in spite of supply officers. The 84th Group was desperately short of buses, cars, tires, nails, lumber, tarpaper to build barracks for pilots (to keep them from getting colds which quickly lead to suffocation in their oxygen masks), pots, pans—in short, all the things one would never suspect an Air Force of needing. Here I became aware that an unspoken implication of my suitability for burglary hung in the air.

"You are welcome to steal from the French, the Canadians, the Americans, even from those callous snails who make up the British Army!"

"Could not the two missions be combined?" I ventured. "Why steal from our friends, the French, the Canadians or the Americans? Isn't it the Germans we are fighting?"

The group captain covered his face. He could not officially condone such flagrant and delightful insubordination. But the spirit of a man who possessed the vision to become an Air Marshall was altogether with me.

For the official record, his statements have been deleted except for his final warning: "No casualties please! It would be unsupportable considering your missions will not have been officially authorized." So I kept my word, even when five of us looked into twenty German muzzles.

My nerves came ajar at the roar of the sergeant when he saw me in a Captain's uniform, "Impersonation of an officer, you cracked imbecile." When I finally succeeded in conveying all the facts he was numbed. "And you took all that gaff from me!"

Everybody fought and pushed to be with us on our lunatic missions. With the pick of the men and the best Air Force truck we penetrated deep into Germany, preceded by a Citroen we had stolen from the French after the French had stolen it back from the Germans who had stolen it from them. The vehicles had neat RAF markings and we were in blue Air Force uniforms. Our only trouble was passing the American sentries on our way back. They never learned our RAF markings either like the Germans, but they were more curious. The Germans had seen so many markings and uniforms issued by a uniform-crazy hierarchy they were completely immune. So, after leaving the last Germans, saluting, we then were hooked by the Provost Marshall's men who subjected me to a gruelling grilling while my men sneaked off with the evidence. Toward the end of the war, five of us encountered one German who was uncomfortably well-informed.

We were looting a tire shop in Kreffeld. We had started knocking boards off a barricaded window when a face appeared on the second floor above us.

"Warten sie doch. Ich komme ja r'unten!"

So we waited until he came r'unten. This man knew at once we were from the RAF. He delayed us by a lot of talk saying that his tires were hardly good enough for the British—only for the German army. We said they would have to do. Then he wanted me to sign for them, which further delayed us. The man talked on, saying nice things about us, while listening, it seemed, expectantly. We busied ourselves stacking tires and patching equipment near the door, ready for loading.

A gleam of triumph suddenly lit up the man's face. He stopped talking and according to international courtesy, we felt at liberty to leave.

The gleam of triumph on our host's face was explained to us as we came out. Our lookouts that we had posted outside were staring unenthusiastically into twenty German muzzles. A German Sergeant leading this welcoming party asked me, "Are you in charge here?"

I did not deny it. He invited us all to his headquarters.

My instructions were clear: no casualties. Were prisoners casualties? Hang it all, nobody had ever told me! If I refused to go along and we all got shot, wouldn't we be more definite casualties? The Air Force code says: when in doubt, seek the best counsel available. That, I presumed, would be Johnson, just over from the Norwegian underground. If you survive in the underground, you have brains. Besides, I had so recently been a private I had learned to respect the brain power of my fellow-privates.

"Johnson, what do we do now?"

Like all great men, Johnson abhorred hurry. First he scratched his three-year-old beard. The Germans pulled their triggers a bit tighter. My men watched those triggers—all but Johnson, who watched the sky, and myself, who watched Johnson. "Well," drawled Johnson unhurriedly, "ask that bloody Sergeant what he's having for supper tonight."

I couldn't see any immediate solution to our pressing problem in this strictly social inquiry but just to please Johnson, I asked it.

The German Sergeant's expression slipped from gloating to bewilderment, then to anger. He spat, "Cabbage soup, as usual, I guess; why?"

I sent Johnson a look of wonderment and gratitude for now I understood the ingenious working of the superior mind. From then on I was able to carry on on my own.

Vibrating with sympathy, I addressed the German:

"Sergeant, not that we don't appreciate your kind invitation to share your cabbage soup tonight but, this being Wednesday and thus steak day back at our Air Force barracks, I was just thinking…"

At this point the Sergeant straightened into a formidable pose. There was a new and vibrant fury on his face. But the twenty muzzles of his men drooped.

"I just passed the Americans at the city gate," I went on, "they are advancing like a steamroller; so are the British to the north. You have been fighting a heroic battle but why expose your men to inevitable death this late in the day? Why not make sure that you all will come home to your wives and children — after a short time with us?"

My last words had bounced off the backs of the twenty hungry men and their Sergeant. They were on their way already.

As I trotted along behind them I was suddenly assailed by gnawing doubt. I had invited my German guests for the Wednesday night steak at our Air Force Camp. But according to the capricious rules of war I would have to give them up to the first Allied unit we reached. We were in the area of the American Ninth Army. Would my promise of steak be honoured?

The American Sergeant looked the twenty over.

"For the love a' Mike," he fumed "I think I'll let 'em go!"

"At least not until you have fed them steak," I protested firmly, explaining to the Sergeant my solemn promise as a British officer. Oratorically I launched into a lecture on the Allied cause, justice and the honouring of treaties.

"Steak for that bunch!" snorted the American. He underscored his derision by tossing a batch of K-rations at the prisoners.

Upon the Germans Sergeant's face one could divine the shaping of a coming Hitler.

Chapter 12

A Welcome Turned TERROR

Whence comes this bursting urge to find and show, in all its gruesome detail, my most terrifying experience of World War II?

Was it went five of us gazed gloomily down the wrong ends of twenty German muzzles suggestively pointed at us?

Or was it when, in the company of three suavely conversing British spies, I heard that stentorian "HALTE!" midway across a bridge and saw 22 precision rifles trained on us?

Or was it that night in Elverum when I saw a little girl's head stick up out of the rubble in that bombed out house, and the light in her eyes went out?

No I think the greatest horror, the craziest jump from bliss to livid TERROR was in that bed in Brussels where I first thought I was being given a giant hero-welcome.

American and British infantry had overrun the city the day before, driven out the remaining Nazis and then left. The smouldering gratitude of the liberated Brusselois was thus reserved for us of the Royal Air Force who arrived undangerously in the wake of the hero-chumps. Four deliriously happy girls took charge of my humble person in a substitute hero welcome such as I shall never forget—but I did forget my last bus to camp.

Three of my fair sponsors could only offer their sincere sympathy. The fourth had a solution:

"You can stay with us!"

"You—really have a room to spare?"

"With a bed!" She added happily.

When we arrived at her home and she showed me the room

and the bed, I was impressed. It was the longest, widest bed I had ever laid eyes on. She smiled good night and left. No sooner had I undressed and crawled in than the door discreetly opened and the girl re-entered. With her eyes modestly turned floorwards, she silently undressed and crawled in beside me.

I edged over to the other side of the bed being naturally modest, and also because of my father's advice to my friends and self on the occasion of my 11th birthday party, "Gentlemen, I recommend monogamy!"

The girl took no offence nor did she make any counter move. She seemed utterly content.

There was a sharp knock on the door.

"Who is that?" I rasped

The girl looked rapturously happy as if now the top of the evening had arrived.

"Oh," she chirped, "that is my husband, Jacques—he will be so happy to meet you!

As the husky smiling Belgian entered, the girl announced, "Jacques, dear, this is Bryn, a liberator and hero—Bryn, meet my husband, Jacques!"

Jacques bowed and scraped, flushed with excitement over the honour of entertaining a liberating hero, then undressed and crawled in on the other side of the fair lady.

While my nerves were still clanking and cracking, raw and exposed, there was another sound, far mightier, as of an avalanche approaching the door. Had the Nazis returned?

In stormed an army of shouting terrors.

"Bryn," beamed the lady, pride in her eyes and voice, "Meet Anton and Greta and Mary and Stomp." Whereupon Anton and Greta and Mary and Stomp threw their clothes on the floor and jumped into bed with us, their parents and hero-guest.

Chapter 13

Gore

News seeped out from Hitler's tribunals and jails that made it difficult to breathe, or even think. Allied brains 5000 miles away had decided against our plan to help the Germans get rid of a nightmare. So, these anti-Nazi Germans, who could have helped us establish and run a worthy postwar world, decided, in desperation, to try on their own. Everyone with the slightest knowledge of modern organization and weaponry knows that such an effort is almost certain to fail without outside help, there is nothing a group of dissenters can do against totalitarian governments today, even if these dissenters are in a majority. These Germans knew this better than anybody. They nevertheless decided to bet on the desperately slim chance of succeeding. Rather die, these courageous men said, then live under a shameless, destructive regime.

So Count Stauffenberg, at that time holding valid credentials in the Hitler entourage, came to a meeting with a briefcase carrying a bomb. A guard wanted to check the contents at the door. The Count laughed him off and entered. He placed the briefcase on the floor beside his chair, only feet away from Hitler.

Count Stauffenberg had taken a suicidal risk bucking the elaborate security system and he is reported seriously to have considered blowing himself up along with Hitler, to be sure of success. In the last minute, however, he drummed up some excuse and walked out, leaving the briefcase close to Hitler. Just before the bomb went off, Hitler also left his place, got out of lethal reach but was badly burned when the bomb went off, though still sufficiently alive to sic his men on a hunt for the "guilty," and there were many.

All through the military cadres, through the civil service, through every department, faithful rebels had for months been preparing for the complete takeover at the moment Hitler would be gone. Every person even remotely connected with these preparations was rounded up and jailed, not for a later trial, as in America, but for continual torture, to reveal the names of others implicated and, in addition, to satisfy the unholy lust of the lunatic sadists in the Hitler hierarchies.

There was an Army Captain, a brilliant organizer, who had been sitting up nights working out the enormous jigsaw puzzle, and could have escaped but doggedly worked on until caught. He was beaten with chains until his kidneys were crushed. Then a voluptuous girl torturer approached him, glistening with lust, the forefinger and little finger of her right hand held high, to be thrust into the captain's two eyes, extinguishing them forever.

After months of this type of treatment, the captain was mercifully hanged, to provide room for a new victim.

Others were treated to hot enemas, hotter and hotter until the victims felt death coming and would tell all, and more. At the last boiling treatment, death would relieve their suffering. This invention was exported and used on Czech and Norwegian patriots, to make them reveal secrets of the anti-Nazi underground, or invent secrets when they had none to tell. Walter Klaussen, our Fire Chief friend from the previous chapter, secretly removed corpses of Norse patriots thus treated, before they were to be burned to wipe out evidence. A victim of this type of torture, who had survived, told me that at first he did not think he could stand the pain. He was ready to babble off names and accusations. Then he realized that half the pain was fear of death. He stopped fearing death and felt only half the pain.

For the chief actors in the drama, Count Stauffenberg and his close associates, a different type of treatment was reserved. They were torn limb from limb, beginning with the toes, fingers, then arms, legs—slowly, lasting for days. It has been said that Hitler himself watched this scene from time to time and that the screams of the victims seemed to be music to his ears.

During their ordeal, during this suffering beyond comprehension, would Count Stauffenberg or his co-victims ever have thought about the handful of Americans across the Atlantic, who unwittingly had contributed to their fate by refusing the outside and essential help proposed to achieve their goal?

This speculation is not entered here to gloat over the ignorance or callousness of men who have now passed away but hopefully to prevent a repetition of such action or inaction in the future. That Americans, of all people, look with such respect at a self-installed "head of state" and consider him representative of a people who never voted for him is so amazing that the tragedy of it is not at first evident. Every four years we watch the dubious game of presidential elections yet, these elected officials are 1000 times more representative of the people's wishes and ideas than such as Hitler and his "rise to power" through threats, murders and blackmail techniques.

We are talking and writing even today about "non-interference" in the affairs of another nation as if we talked about a single person's life while it should be obvious to all that "interference" of the most wanton and cruel kind was practised daily by the Hitler gang against Germans, as it is still practised by many governments against their citizens.

Gautama fled his father's palace, rejected his heritage and all hierarchies and taught the dignity and sacredness of individual man. His followers, at his death, created a new and oppressive hierarchy of monks and priests of various degrees and ranks in stark contrast to him who they revered. That son of a carpenter in ancient Palestine rejected the kingship his followers tried to bestow upon him and he, also, taught the dignity of man to a group of fishermen and artisans, and to the rich and poor, and he did not show much respect for the civil or religious hierarchy. After his death his servants re-established oppressive hierarchies of monks, priests, bishops, cardinals and pope, defying everything their professed ideal stood for.

And not long ago, presidents and generals of the United States respected a rascal who seized power in Germany—respected him to such an extent that they identified him with a great German people and refused to help when the German people themselves asked for help to rid themselves of the horror. Calmly they saw a people torn limb from limb, slowly; they listened unmoved to the screaming, sermonizing that the "Germans must be beaten so they know it."

Eric Hoffer, the former longshoreman who now is a lecturer at the University of California recently told about a highway project in the San Bernardino mountains east of Los Angeles where they had difficulty finding workers. They sent two trucks down to skid row in Los Angeles, picked up willing men in the streets and parks, took them to the site, provided tools and camping equipment, explained what was to be done, then left the crowd alone. A beautiful highway was built in minimum of time. No hierarchy.

Henry Ford I, our first real industrial organizer, used to say, "A group of Americans usually can do a fine job together, except when they form a hierarchy. That spoils it."

About the time during World War II that Hitler's form of revenge became known to us, a development began that was in many respects the total contrast. Groups of Belgians, and, later, Dutch civilians offered their services to us as workers. We knew none of them and time was short. We acted just like the San Bernardino highway management: let them work, without forming any hierarchy, any "organization". They accepted this arrangement with great pleasure and ingenious adaptation. When barracks were to be built, carpenters and masons among them came forward and guided the work, with the rest as helpers. When plumbing was called for, the plumbers came forward and the others reverted to general helpers.

Once a British Army Engineering unit came along to an airfield where such a Belgian crew was working. The RAF commander now had a choice between two work forces to complete some strips and barracks in a hurry. He first asked the Army Engineers, who after lengthy deliberations said they could do the work in two weeks. Then he asked the Belgians who it once said four days would be all right. They did it in three and a half.

The slavish attachment to hierarchies among many Germans prior to World War II was a strong contributing factor to the gory

Hitler reign over a highly civilized nation. Hitler was not even German. He was Austrian—which is not to say that Austrians are like him. Of whatever nationality he was, he was an exception. His German followers were just that: followers, not gory sadists—not generally. Even the notorious SS troops were often courteous, well-behaved, good conversationalists and you could frequently bribe them with good food, wine and animated company. One of my friends who was married to a rich and charming German noblewoman got out of jail by her wiles with the SS guards.

But Hitler, like a gangland mobster, drew the scum of a nation around him (his equals) and these took charge and dominated the others and the whole nation. And this gangster turned Head of State, was accepted by our American counterparts who saw him as representing the fine German nation, thus causing the best Germans to become dismembered in screaming agony.

Chapter 14

Spies are Beautiful

Karl Meyer, a decent, respectable German economist from Hanover, arrived in London on a passport manufactured by his Gestapo espionage school and sporting the name of an English soldier who had died from wounds in a secret Gestapo hideout.

The first thing Karl Meyer did when he came to London was to open an account with the Post Office Savings Bank at Charing Cross. After that he lay low, ate, slept and waited for instructions. A whole week went by with sightseeing and locating possible targets or victims. Then, at eight one evening there was a knock at the door. Karl opened the door himself and faced two young men who weren't smiling. They asked him politely to come along for questioning.

There weren't many questions asked. The British Security Police seemed to know everything about him already; his background, his espionage training.

Karl Meyer was not too perturbed. He knew from his espionage teachers that the British did not torture captured spies, not anymore. At most they were shot. Also, there was a good chance of some mutually profitable solutions, such as switching bosses. Karl Meyer had thought this through many times before he hopped over to London. He was a man of the world; was ready to serve a master other than German. But he feared the consequences if he were sent back to spy on his countrymen. In Germany he risked not only death but very unpleasant treatment before death would relieve him.

First, however, he was beset by curiosity. "Why," he asked, "did you find out about me so quickly, even before anyone had contacted me?"

"Our first indication," responded the security police, "was your opening of an account in the Post Office Savings Bank. Of course many open such accounts even though they are not spies. We investigate all of them. "

"But why? Why? Our Gestapo teacher told us to open such accounts as soon as possible after arrival. This, he told us, would be taken as a sign that we were solid British citizens acting as they would have done."

"Yes," replied the security police, "because that Gestapo espionage teacher is our agent."

The policeman who made this statement was soon removed because of his indiscretion. In his defence he said he was so sure that Karl Meyer would be shot before dawn that he saw no danger in satisfying Karl's curiosity. His superiors countered that it was his own sensationalism he satisfied rather than the other's curiosity. Besides, Karl Meyer was not shot at dawn. He became a British agent. He was captured by the German security police and at once offered to switch back to become a German agent again. The Germans were not generous. They treated him in unmentionable ways, then shot the rest of him.

Karl Meyer became my dream hero in London, or rather my object of envy, that is, before I knew what finally happened to him in Germany. Why hadn't I thought of going to a German spy school before landing in England? I would have been so much more useful in the battle against Hitler, I mused—that is, if the English hadn't shot me at dawn before I had time to explain myself.

Two men changed all that in seconds by merely exercising their tonal chords. A Royal Air Force General said, "Come with us," and sent me to the Western Front to a Royal Air Force Group Captain (now an Air Marshall) who sent me behind German lines. I did not have the protection of a mighty army, not even the less sure shield of an intelligence organization. I was, with my buddies, a tramp, a non-entity, open to all the tortures the Nazis could think of if they caught me. We, my buddies and I, felt great now, greater than the army or the Air Force; greater even than the regular spies, for we were farther out; out of bounds; out of all Geneva convention; all human or inhumane systems. We were on our own, as the Stone Age cavemen before us. Every time I made one of my forays into enemy territory either to find a lost pilot or to steal a bus or a coffee pot, I could pick any one of my company fellows. They all wanted to go, wanted to become part of our lawless gang. Yes, spies are beautiful but super-spies beyond all bonds and reasons are beautifuller.

I had expected that my occupation as a super-or-sub spy would cease at the end of World War II and that I would then revert to a more respectable engineer and past-jackaroo. This was not to be. To the straining embarrassment of the CIA, the CIS, the SCI, all military intelligence units, the entire G-2, Colonel Carroll, E.F. Nelson, the Pentagon and even my humble self, I was taken for a member of any or all these various organizations or buildings wherever I popped up in the world.

In Japan this turned tragic for there I really intended to practice the old art again. I stayed with loveable Colonel Nelson of G-2 and planned a trip to Blagovashenck to see what the Russies were doing while we all were waiting for that thrust across a certain border.

To stay with the Nelsons was a privilege I wouldn't have swapped for a king's ransom so I was upset when one evening the Colonel barked, "Why did you tell Major Frye you were of the CIA?"

We went right over to see Major Frye together. He was an "operator", a real beautiful spy in the field and though I would have been proud to really be of the CIA, I was greatly upset that such a fine specie should be misinformed about me. Major Frye put on his most winning smile and addressed himself to the Colonel, "No, no, Colonel; I never said Bryn had said he was of the CIA. He is highly discrete and would never have said such a thing. Our knowledge is from other sources."

The Colonel gave up. "When such rumours start," he said, "the best you can do a shut up. The more you deny, the bigger become the rumours."

The local representative of the US State Department categorically refused to let me go on my mission to Blagovashenk, so carefully planned by the beautiful people. I had to try from another base. That is how I met Ivanshenko in Hong Kong, after the military attaché had obtained for me an extension of my stay permit by phoning the British passport office that I wished to stay on a bit longer "for personal reasons." A private mission plane brought me to the heart of China and back.

Have these — my various and not-too-impressive spy credentials —entitled me to stand in awe before that super-spy who reached higher into space and deeper into mind sophistication than any other spy, Francis Gary Power? In Russia he played the repentant sinner and told them nothing of the secrets he knew, and back in America the knowledgable men who could have benefitted from his trek did not even see him or were not allowed to. I know I would have bungled the court scene in Moscow. I would have pretended to go along in the preparations. In the court itself, faced with a world audience, I would have said, "Gentlemen, spies are the most beautiful people, the cream of nations, as your Stalin already said to Roosevelt at Yalta and here you set up a mock court to judge and insult the people who risked their all for your safety! Are you nuts or something?" And before I could finish even this preliminary opening, I would have been shot from behind by a silenced gun and the court physician would have proclaimed: "Heart failure due to the sinner's guilt feelings."

Powers did better than that. He kept his opinions to himself and played his role like a real beautiful pro, nobly ignoring the ridiculous antics around him to the very end, and so gained his release and returned to his country where the big shots understood little of his plight and wisdom, for they did not seek his counsel. Not even the biggest shots can fully appreciate a beautiful spy—the salt of the earth, the saviour of nations and the world.

An incident in the first World War shows what people in the know think a good spy is worth. Admiral Jellico, on the bridge of the British flagship in the battle of Jyllland, was approached via messenger who joyfully reported that the German battle cruiser Scharnhorst had been sunk. No survivors. The Admiral received this message with a drawn face,

"Damn it, Scharnhorst's first mate was our best agent."

Not even a huge battle cruiser with thousands of able-bodied officers and sailors were comparable to one single beautiful spy.

Chapter 15

I Conquer Bardenberg

The airman is just a pepper shaker. And he knows it. He peppers the enemy, burying it for the infantry to eat. And an airman's aide, who supports and hardens him and upon his shoulder he may weep or cry? What is he? Why, he is just a pepper shakers pepper maker!

Neither ever conquered! Neither ever swaggered!

What wonder then, when fighter pilot Ed and I were granted a vacation, that we should seek release and happiness in the arms of the infantry? Fight and conquer? Eat what we had peppered?

Though for Ed and I, in our state of mind, just any infantry would not have been good enough. We were to fight alongside the champion of the world: the USA! For Ed, to get away from neck-breaking pepper shaking and I, from reputation-breaking pepper makings, clowning along the Rhine.

In a Citroen we had stolen from the Germans who in turn had stolen it from the French, we set out. The night between October 10 and 11th we bunked at a house on the outskirts of Bardenburg, on the road to Cologne, barely a mile from the front line. The monotony of grinding vehicles and artillery firing lulled us to sleep. Toward midnight, however, the noise grew to a hurricane of sounds. Above the shooting was heard the grinding of a thousand wheels. I went out into the pitch black night in the drenching rain and asked of a dim red light, "Is this advance—or retreat?"

"Retreat?" came a southern voice from out of the night, drawn out like a rubber sheet. "Have you ever seen Americans retreat since we landed in France the sixth of June?"

Ed had joined me, and under a flashlight we showed our papers while walking along at the leisurely pace of the night convoy.

"Hop in!" drawled the southerner, "The more the merrier!"

We parked outside the town. The General's car was already there, empty. He had continued on foot into town. Our Lieutenant host with the southern drawl offered us infantry helmets. I gratefully accepted but Ed insisted on wearing his pilot's cap. So we advanced, our Lieutenant flanked by we two guests and his walkie-talkie man close on our heels. We crossed a field, swampy, soaked with rain. A herd of cattle looked us over dubiously, then expressed their feeling about us in a unison moo. This must've been a signal, for at that very moment the first German 155 mm shell sang and then burst. They followed at 20 second intervals and closed in. We learned to discern the hiss of the shell as it passed, whether it was left, right, short, long, or right on.

A neat little brick house—a doctor's combined residence and office—was hardly an appropriate shelter but in a basement garage was a shiny new Opel which the doctor had left behind when he fled. Ed, like all pilots, loved cars and he couldn't stand the thought of this beauty being molested by a 155 shell so he jumped through a basement window to be with his love while we others went on our business.

Some strange trees, wide around the hips, which we had admired from a distance, began to move. They were our tanks. They fell in line, humbly, behind the infantry front line. German civilians looked at us and we at them. They looked tired and hungry. Many stared past us as if we were pure air. Were they showing the same contempt for the conquerors that I had seen the Norwegians show for the German occupation forces? There was a difference. As guest actors, Ed and I could afford to smile at them tentatively. They immediately responded, overwhelmingly.

They became talkative: They called their Nazi compatriots "die braune pest." They told us the local Nazi leaders had taken along the young and healthy when the town was evacuated, except for military defenders, and had abandoned the rest, and added insult to injury by shouting at them, "You are Germans no longer, you are traitors—scum!"

The cooperation of these people went further. Some of them eagerly offered to show us the minefields and how to maneuver through them. We responded by asking any such volunteer to go across, and show us. They did. We followed. There was never an accident.

Why? Did these people really look at us as liberators? Or were they only playing up to whomever they considered strongest at the moment? Who would be bold enough or foolish enough to make generalizations? Obviously both types existed, and many other shades of mind.

We had reached that hot ground where intelligence had placed the German positions. Drunk with excitement I asked a G.I. in a doorway, "Where is the front?"

A not too bright question in the circumstances, inviting an acid reply, but the G.I. answered evenly, "I guess I am it!"

A bit further ahead, near the center of this charming town, where a skyscraper ought to have loomed, was, instead, a fertile farm, and out of the farmhouse came now a huge apparition waving both arms at us. What did he want? Give information or set a trap?

Through some deliberation I decided that, being a guest, my life and fate were about the cheapest available. I went up to him. He pointed to a dark brick house further up the street.

"Germanische soldaten," he said, "are in that house. If you try to attack through this street you will be mowed down whereas through my farm you may advance unnoticed and surprise him."

I pondered his words; not the least his term "Germanische" instead of "Deutsche". Did he wish to hint at the difference between the genuine Deutsche (German) spirit and the Germanische suggesting racial gibberish? Or did he know the English word for Deutsch was 'German' and did he think we would understand that term better?

I went with him through his farm and saw how we could reach the German base. The Americans agreed to send a small patrol with me through the farm. Many more volunteered than we could take along.

When I reached that farmhouse again I was fascinated by a sign

I had not seen before. It was fastened to the wall and read, "On this farm Germans have lived and toiled for many hundred years. It will therefore, like all other farms and town houses in Germany, form an unbreakable bulwark against any intruder." Obviously this farmer did not consider the Allied forces intruders.

Through the farm, the capture of the first German stronghold became a neat operation. The Germans were surprised and all were taken prisoner. No raw mutilating!

From the stronghold that had been German and now had become American we had a grandstand view of the American penetration. The thrusts of advancing lines in many directions following an almost perfect geometric pattern became a living graph of expert planning and meticulous execution. Our painless capture of the first stronghold had put the timetable ahead.

Still there were casualties. An American positioned on the steps of a church opposite the farm through which we had come, crouched and fell, blood gushing from his head, obviously hit by a sniper on the opposite side of the street. All these houses had been searched. A renewed search brought out from a basement a white-faced little man who immediately yelled at the top of his lungs,

"I am no soldier; I am just a peaceful baker—baker, you got me? I have eight innocent little children, eight! Do you hear?"

A sergeant padded him on the back. "Take it easy, Pop. Let's have a load of your cream puffs and show us your naughty kids!"

The man's lips trembled. He had been told, he said, that Americans summarily shot all prisoners of war!

"I understand," said I, "that you have six tanks in town?"

"Haw!" puffed the German, "if we had had six tanks you would have had a different reception! We have only four kraftspahwagen!"

"You know pretty much for a peaceful baker," bellowed the sergeant. The German bit his lip.

Our advance forced the Germans out of their covered positions into the streets. Now American eagles dived at these moving targets. The German air defences responded. Red tracers lit up the dark clouds; black patches dotted the sky.

The Germans, repositioned, opened intensive mortar fire that cut almost in half a house we were just planning to enter. Well, chances are slim that particular house would be hurt again, we reasoned, so we entered and were met with a hail of new shells, all duds!

Texas Jim, the big non-com who never could leave a good thing alone, set about to peel one dud, layer after layer, amid our howls of nervous protest, and finally found, in the innermost sanctum, a piece of thin, oily paper with bold letters, "Greetings from Czechoslovakia!"

This emboldened us to venture out into the streets for a further advance, which was met by a drumfire of machine gun bullets. Flying pieces of brick loosened by the bullets hammered our helmets. The fire came from a brick house a few hundred feet further up the street. We sought shelter within a walled yard again and felt we had to come too close and with insufficient strength—sensed with that ESP which great men share—or was the word FEAR? Was our duty now to storm that brick house? Hum, well, wasn't that for the tanks? And where were the tanks? Hiding behind Mama's skirt? Texas Jim peeked over the wall and saw the Germans file out of the building, poised for counter attack! These, obviously, were trained assault troops. At least 50 of them. And we? Six raw recruits, one guest from the British Air Force, and Texas Jim. A fair match?

The raw recruits were beginning to pale, so Texas Jim regaled us with a blood-stained tale of the battle of Valley Forge and gestured meaningfully to the brick walls around us: Why the walls of the old fort!

The lookout on the wall facing the street called out,

"Drunk approaching from 12 o'clock on five!"

I peeked over his shoulder and there, up the street, came a man reeling, stumbling from one side of the street to the other and wearing the largest helmet I had ever seen (like an upside down bucket) completely covering his face. Both his reeling movements and the size of his helmet had so far saved him from the effects of a murderous machine gun fire except that pieces of brick torn loose by the bullets drummed on his helmet at a fabulous pitch.

Then there was a sudden inspiration—or was it revelation? I knew this man. He was my pal Ed who had sworn he would never exchange his Air Force cap for a helmet and who, furthermore, must have succeeded, temporarily at least, in tearing himself loose from a brand new Opel. We shouted to him. One of his rally thrusts threw him right through our gate and into our laps.

"Had to see how you were doing," he stated.

Well, our force had been increased by twenty percent. But the Germans were still coming. We looked at our bayonets. Where were those tanks? Never where you needed them!

Mingling irreverently with our accusing voices was a nasty noise down the street, a crushing grind as if the pavement was ripped up by a mechanical jack-the-ripper. The dragon didn't make haste but oh, did it advance! The electrifying effect was not only on us, but on the Germans, too. For some tense seconds all firing stopped, all enemy advance ceased, all noise quieted except that heavy grind.

Texas Jim and I waved to the tank and as it reached the gate to our yard the top flew open and a captain popped up and out. The Germans had been swept from the street but machine guns again rattled with renewed frenzy. We showed the tank commander the German stronghold. He jumped back in, closed the hatch and the tank moved forward again. Texas Jim and I walked along, our hands on the gun muzzle as if we were leading a horse, to be sure he didn't miss the place. Bullets rained about us but we were too dumb to be hit.

The tank stopped. The muzzle moved down and sideways. Machine gun bullets splattered frustratingly on the tank armour.

"Boom-wranghh!"

Three times the gun recoiled. Three gaping holes showed in the German Headquarters building. There was no machine gun fire.

As we were grouped for the mop-up, a new face appeared on the scene. He wore an American uniform and a coat over his tunic. No insignia of rank was visible. His face grew purple as he looked Ed and me over.

"Who are you? Who the hell are you!! ?"

It was only then I realized our dark blue RAF uniforms must stand out, colour wise, against the US khaki.

"You are a bit late for the best part of the show now," suggested

Ed. This reply did not mellow the newcomer.

Loudly he repeated, "Who are you!"

"We are from the RAF sir. I assume you are the Captain of…"

"Major!" He snapped, "I thought the RAF had some business up there (he looked at the sky) rather than wasting time playing infantryman and endangering our advance!"

"Endangered, my hat!" broke in Texas Jim, "Here these two crazy RAF men spend their much-deserved vacation cheering up your boys, Major, and you go sour on them! Now if you are to stop us from having any fun in this unfunny war, I, for one, might just as well go home!"

I showed the Major our papers. There was an inkling of a grin on his sober face as he mumbled "Carry-on!" Then he turned and left.

The Captain of M company under whom our Lieutenant-host served invited me to a grand tour of the front. This was a great honour which I accepted with thanks. We zigzag-leaped across streets with barricades thrown up around cracked pavements and over two dead horses, their legs pointing stiffly into the air. Machine gun bullets were flying—from where? When we arrived in the the safety of a G.I. stronghold a Corporal patted us on our backs.

"Lucky babies."

The bullets, we found, came from a house where a man in a G.I. tunic was firing. We threw a hand grenade into the house. White cloth came up. A woman appeared. The German in the G.I. tunic (was it her husband?) was dead.

We had to go through a farm with a complicated pattern of fences and pathways to reach the next unit. I lost track of my Captain but he came back for me.

"I am ashamed," I said. "You shouldn't have risked your life and your mission for the sake of a crazy RAF guest."

"You have done as much as any of us, "he said. "You are one of us now and we are responsible for each other."

The fine-combing of all houses to finish the job and list the city as conquered was organized by a Sergeant specialist just out of the hospital. He had been told to stay at least three weeks in that hospital for healing of a leg wound. He insisted on getting out after four days. Now he was "back with the boys," a veteran American infantryman, the greatest in the world.

It was weeks later when the American Colonel asked me to write a report.

"Report?"

My heart dropped down into my belly. Here I thought we had had a good time, a real vacation, and now this Colonel made it out to be just another military routine job. A report!

It wasn't my first bout with the Americans. I had been attached for three months to the 820th Aviation Engineer Battalion, three more months to a service engineering regiment. The Colonel wanted a combined report for my entire US Forces career. He wanted more than that. He wanted a comparison of the American servicemen with the British, the Russian, the German and the Norwegian. He wanted a penetrating analysis, criticism, appreciation.

I began thinking about it. My thinking crackled. I saw, in retrospect, the free, easy-going and incomparably efficient American soldier, airman and sailor. I began to write. The typewriter shrieked. Out came a new version of an old story about one American and one German General sitting high in the Alps discussing their men's discipline.

The German said, "If I say to one of them, 'jump from this precipice' he will jump!"

The American said, "If I should be fool enough to say that to one of our soldiers, he would drawl, 'who do you think you are?' And that, General, is why we won this war and all other wars we have waged!"

Although a Lieutenant General slapped my back in appreciation, I have begun to have second thoughts. In a civilized battle area like this German front, my report may be valid. A different evaluation was provided by Lin Piauo after the first clash between American and (his own) Chinese troops in North Korea in 1950. First he gives the Americans credit for superior firing power and range, exquisite communications and transportation systems. Then:

"Cut off from the rear, the Americans abandon their heavy weapons. Their infantry men are afraid to die and have little taste for either attacking or defending, leaving such chores to planes, tanks, artillery. They are not familiar with night fighting or hand-to-hand combat. When defeated they retain no orderly formation. Without the use of their mortars they become lost, dazed, demoralized. When their rear is cut off and transportation comes to a standstill, they lose all will to fight."

Whatever Lin Piauo may have seen in Korea that prompted this early report made him raring to fight Americans again and the reports he received from Vietnam egged on this desire to a mania to take on the "dazed and demoralized Americans." In this desire he became so unmanageable he had to be disposed of, as the music of the THAW was played by greater minds.

Chapter 16

Nothing Ever Happens Up There

Permission to fly with American B-24s over Germany came through so fast I suspected the Ninth US Army had lent a hand, to get me out of the hair of its infantry for a few days, at least. It was the same Ninth Army that eagerly provided me with a ride from the Western Front to the 452nd Bomber Group in England.

Arriving, I was warned that passengers were not wanted, nor were tourists. A fortune had been spent training the crew. These expensive lives were not to be jeopardized by some ignorant nut fooling with the equipment.

Shaken, crushed, I croaked with a voice I no longer recognized, weird remnants left in the deep recesses of my respiratory chambers, that I was not a tourist, not a passenger but a member of the crew and that I hoped to be useful, nay, indispensable, and would insist on submitting to rigorous training that might make me worthy of such expensive fellow crewmen. Stern features dissolved into smiles and I was put through the mill. A thousand and one gadgets had to be studied, mastered, safety devices disassembled and reassembled, rubber boats inflated and the Mae West, with happiest side thoughts about its taut lady namesake; a mast to be put together and raised, a boat engine to be serviced and started; use of a morphine syringe; swallowing of dried milk tablets, loading and shooting signal flares; handling the waist gun, getting a whiff of navigation, radio, maintenance, parachutes; a course in the prisoner-of-war code and how to get back home if you jumped. Finally the crowning test: Altitude!

A four-engine giant with a crew of five just for me! In mighty spirals they lifted me up—10,000 feet, 15,000. They looked at me sideways, seeming pleasantly surprised I was still alive. They put on me an oxygen mask. Its light blinked yellow for each breath, like a shrewd conspirator. Outside was soft snow. An Easter Sunday in the Norse mountains! I would have liked to roll out into it but the doors were too firmly closed. 20,000, 25,000. Someone pointed at the waist gun. I went through the loading and aiming motions. It made me so tired my knees buckled. The pants were wide so it didn't show. The snow under us was far below now, too far to roll down into.

In large spirals we descended again. The crew looked at me as medics do, kindly and unfeelingly, and seemed absorbed by the fact that I was still alive. Pleasantly absorbed.

"He made it, didn't he? "

At 2:30 the following morning we ate powdered eggs, bacon and buckwheat cakes. Thus fortified, some of us managed to stay awake during the briefing hours. Goal for the day: a switchyard behind the Siegfried line. A sigh shivered through the ranks. It had been switchyards behind the Siegfried line for weeks on end! Couldn't those briefing boys ever hit upon anything different? The briefer boy tapped a large wall map with his pointer, showing the target area, the positions (known and assumed) of ack-ack batteries; of fighter strips. We were again told what to do, how to behave if we had to jump; how to try getting back to our own lines.

Pilots, copilot, navigators and bombardiers were retained for further special briefings while the rest of the crew, with selected guests or tourists, were sent off to check out the craft. The pilots and company joined us after their additional three full hours of briefing, their heads full of time schedules on formations, sequence of crafts and their place in formations, signal codes, code names of towns and cities along the way. In our polar jackets, giant boots, pants with pockets all the way down to the ankles, we looked like a forward invasion squadron from Mars.

The engines were started, one after another. Guests' and greenhorns' eyes popped: this was it, wasn't it? We were moving! We looked outside: no, not really. But then the engines were revved up to shattering roaring, so this must be it! Most certainly! Until the thunder abated and we were standing there exactly in the same place, like a baby bird having tried to fly and failed.

Ages later we did move, up to the beginning of the runway, and there we stopped again, starting, revving, stopping; hopes crushed by utter failure! Just as we had settled down to realizing nothing would ever happen, the great bird sneaked cagily out and down that concrete dance floor, so slowly first that you weren't even suspicious, then shooting out, hissing, screaming, heaving and bumping along that rugged product of the 820 Aviation Engineer Battalion. Now we could see the pattern on the tires. We were airborne! For two solid hours we circled the airport, completing formations. Our own craft was the lead bird of one group. One after another the majestic co-birds joined us. Their massive bulks ran up friendly and comfortably, a picture of American group spirit, like the pioneering old-timers who went West in covered wagons. The common goal and purpose, the common might, kept them alive. When marauders threatened, they put their carts in a circle to defend their lives and honour.

Now the same old spirit had forged this fleet of monster birds, products of science and technology—which of themselves can do nothing without that will to work together.

The intercom crackled, "Command Pilot to tail: look over the formation. See if it is complete."

"Tail to Command Pilot: how many should there be?"

"Leaping lizards, don't you know? Look if they are nine or 10!"

"I think I see 12."

"12! Blinking blizzards in a hen basket, where do you get the two spares from?"

The two spares, it was finally discovered, belonged to a neighbouring squadron.

We soared up, far above the snowscape of the day before. The wildest mountain ridges covered the horizon, tremendous blobs of rock overhanging deep ravines, the bewitching world of high altitude clouds and insufficient oxygen. So the masks came on and the current to the closing heaters was switched on for all except the flight engineer who had to run all over the ship, checking. He could only have a whiff here and there where he could find a free outlet for a quick refresher.

I loaded the machine gun and did some jumping about to show I was in top condition. That proved to be a costly show-off. I saw black spots before my eyes and had to sit down. To top the event, I did this sitting in a far corner, being ashamed of my condition and wanting no one to see. If my senses had been operating, I would just have switched on more oxygen as I had been told. I was already off to cuckoo land.

The vagrant, ever-moving flight engineer noticed me and turned on the oxygen. What I thought to have been a few seconds' sleep turned out to have been an hour and a half.

Under us was now Germany. Dark smoke clouds cluttered the sky. Muffled thuds were heard above the engine hum. This was our welcome. It didn't look too threatening until a thundering explosion rocked our plane. The liberator that had been flying right underneath us wasn't anymore. Flack must have turned on the bombs.

For me there was no time for mourning. A strange shape came hurtling toward my window and my waist gun. It screamed like a rocket. From its tail shot a streak of fire. It was small at first but grew like a nightmare and would presently fly right through my window and into me. My machine gun clattered without stopping or even delaying the monster. But Lo! An arrow of speed shot up from below. Its cannon did havoc to the monster's belly. It flew apart with another rocking explosion. The pieces tumbled down, down. We had met and seen destroyed the first German jet fighter. A propeller-driven Messerschmitt attacked from the left. A Mustang finished it.

We reached the target. We, the leading liberator, pulled back the stick for the bomb bay to drop the markers. Bomb doors stuck! Others sailed in and dropped their eggs. Large, gray mushrooms sprung up, joined hands and soon totally covered the target area. An intense light shone through the gray mushrooms: Target on fire! Even though our markers had failed to drop.

Flack thundered and shrieked. Fighters battled over and under us. Apparently unconcerned, one after another of the big birds sailed over the area and dropped their loads. This was a new and enervating realization: it took so long! First you waited ages before you could go in and bomb. After that you waited other aeons before the formations were again complete and you could start on the way home. Why couldn't we just go in and bomb, then streak right out? No! We had to fumble around for an eternity while everything Hitler could drum up sprouted fire and death on us,

At long last noses pointed homeward. The danger had not passed. For us, the once-leading liberator, it had increased, for with our bomb load still intact we were heavier than the others and lagged behind, prey to all the fighters that had now a lighted, ready to attack enforce, supported by a continent of flack! The sky was gray and black with ugly smoke whirls. Still, our tense mood from the outward trip was in happy dissolution. One more of the missions required of a bomber crew had been completed—or would be very soon, we all believed. The intercom exuding brief, concise orders and explanations on the outbound trip, now overflowed with wit.

"Look at that windmill—just like one back in Kansas City."

"Is that what you have in Kansas City? I knew there were windbags, not windmills."

"Pilot to Norwegian Captain: Howdy Captain!"

"I'm doing fine, Pilot; learning new words all along!"

"Enjoying your trip?"

"Looking forward to my next one!"

Under us was a Holland faithfully copied from our maps. Then came the North Sea. The Command pilot walked and crawled through the ship explaining to all that he wanted to make one more try to drop the bombs—right down into the sea. He added that even if we didn't succeed, he had seen ships landing safely with a stuck bombload before.

"Says you!" yelped a doubting gunner out of a twisted snout.

The pilot looked at him, "And—what do you say?" That ended the argument.

In leisurely spirals we circled down upon the home field. Things looked small and dear and familiar down there except for a flurry of firetrucks and ambulances and people running—and all because of us! I remembered at that moment that *The Man Who Came to Dinner* would be shown in the movie room that night. That I would have to see, so I knew we would live.

From the playful air element we sailed victoriously in onto firm, trustworthy concrete, making fools of all the eager, nervous fire and first aid men. An hour later we were shown photos of a switchyard behind the Siegfried line—or of what was left of it.

Everybody was depressed because of the ten from the busted liberator who were no longer with us. But flyers cannot mourn for long.

"Oh, hell!" said Fred our tail gunner, "we'll meet the lot of 'em safe and sound soon enough, and with gleaming hero-blobs like Billy's!"

The story of Billy runs the round of the Air Force messes and is picked up polished and served anew every time it is required. Billy was a tail gunner on a liberator that blew up just like the one today. After the explosion Billy found himself soaring through space. The parachute harness was properly fastened on him and the parachute itself was in his hands. He put it on and pulled the string—it was an old-fashioned one of the "it doesn't mean a thing if you don't pull the string" type.

Soon he saw under him a line of attacking troops interspersed with large gray monsters. He dropped right down on one of those monsters and noticed with due appreciation that it was an American tank. In the ensuing battle he demonstrated such bravery "beyond the call of duty" that he became one of the few Americans to receive the Congressional Medal of Honor while still alive.

"This is the life!" shouted Billy. "Nothing ever happens up here!" So who can say a flyer does not have a chance?

Chapter 17

That Coming War

After seven months of burglary I began to panic. Would I ever go straight? Where would I fit in, when breaking and entering would again be frowned upon?

I had loved my role as a land pirate; Robin Hood of the Rhine Shores looting from the Germans and giving the loot to the poor but worthy RAF. Quietly I was digging my own grave.

Then came the order: report to London! Obviously this megalopolis was just a cover for a new and exciting front.

A tired engine puffed and snorted up to a remote Scottish village. After a cold lunch we were marched to a military depot and equipped with mosquito netting, shorts, tropical helmets. Well, this was February in Scotland. A chunk of tropical heat would be acceptable. All the spies in the village took note and dropped messages in invisible ink in hollow trees.

In the middle of the night, with not a soul or nary a spy in the streets of that peaceful little village, we were marched back to that depot again carrying all our tropical gear and exchanging it for skis, ski boots, hooded parkas and heavy wool socks. With our new gear we were loaded on a little train for the coast and while the night was still young, we boarded the HMS Premier anchored near Ayl in the outer part of the Firth of Clyde. The war had converted this lusty sea lady from a cargo-carrying tramp of the American liberty variety to a fighting swan carrying her brood on her back.

As we slid out the Firth slowly, with a minimum of noise and fanfare, we were joined by sleek destroyers, spunky little sub-chasers and 30-odd creaking merchant vessels. We opened and read the sealed orders. Codename CROFTER was to establish headquarters in Kirkenes and sweep the Germans southward. Even though the war crawled toward a happy ending, the Germans in Norway were talking of digging in, not leaving when the Germans on the Continent were defeated and, if pressured, seeing to it that Norway would be reduced to a "scorched earth" before surrendering. The Germans in the south did not speak above a whisper about this. They were too badly harassed by the Norwegian guerrillas on the Hardanger-Vidda. But in the north they boasted of it. We of CROFTER were to stop and close the big mouths. We were to show the Germans what to expect if they tried to carry out their threats of destruction. We took pride in our fierce assignment.

The sailors hadn't read the order and did not know that fierce soldiers were already waiting at Kirkenes for the fierce officer now on their ship. They looked us up and down, feasted their eyes on our brass insignia and and one asked another, "Harry, have you ever seen a Norwegian private?"

The question was repeated down through the decks until the whole ship guffawed. Before long, the whole convoy had heard or seen, by signal lamps, and roared, unmercifully. Well, it was better entertainment than the alternative conversation piece: 38 ships had set out with the preceding convoy; six arrived.

To any sensible submariner our HMS Premier would be the first and prime target, queen of the convoy, riding a bit ahead of center with the destroyers and sub-chasers dancing around us.

Privates or no privates, we were in luck. We arrived at the mouth of the Murmansk Fjord with a load of unused ash cans. The crew told us this was where German subs might be laying for us so we dropped a whole arsenal of cans at once. To me it seemed unlikely subs would be here right under the noses of Russian guns. I thought the crew just hankered to relieve the tension built up during those days at sea.

There was an additional effect. In the double rainbow shown in the glittering geyser from the explosion of the ash cans were thousands of dead fish. Many fell on our deck and provided a welcome change in our diet.

We disembarked at a blacked-out pin dot of a town halfway to

Murmansk. Before the moorings were taut I leaped from the deck. A tight cordon of soldiers with lifted bayonets formed an iron curtain along the land part of the wharf. I found it could be opened most conveniently with packages of cigarettes.

From then on I had freedom of the countryside. I cat-footed my way along muddy streets in pitch-black night until I came upon a square of light framing a man who is singing,

"Hilltops asleep in the darkness of the night,
Silent valleys fill with fresh mist.
There is no dust on the road, no movement of leaves.
Wait, in patience, and rest will come to you, too!"

A flight of stairs led up to the light, a light reaching out through an open door from a mysterious source of hope and gaiety. I mounted the stairs and stopped at the top to watch the singer. He wore the uniform of a Russian army captain. When he had finished his song he came forward with both arms outstretched. It was a Russian way of greeting a guest, a fellow-human. It was an old and fine tradition, so true and genuine it has survived decades of recent theories and dogma. He introduced himself as Ivan Zaizeff. Why, we knew each other!

Zaizeff took me inside—into that mysterious source of hope and gaiety. It was incredible. Must have been an ancient king's palace, though it looked more like a Fata Morgana of the grandest imagination. On a dance floor of polished gold, amid marble columns supporting a ceiling that was one continuous bold artist's dream, high-bosomed girls danced and devoured their partners with eyes that make men climb mountains. A fairy prince's dream! How has such a palace with such girls found its way into this pin dot of a town in the north woods on the shores of an icebound fjord?

Zaizeff dropped down into a deep arm chair and offered me a deeper one. Couples moved over to us and formed a circle around us, singing songs of the steppes. Then they drew up chairs. Conversation came easily, urgently. To an Amerikansky-Norvetchky brother-in-arms they told of life in the woods and on the steppes and what they could make of their great country if only there would be peace! Did I think there would be?

I knew it my bones: peace? Of course there would be peace—and soon!

Oh, they were not talking about the end of this present war. That was coming, they knew. They were thinking of the new war, the coming one—the war that would be started by people who wanted to rule the world!

On my guard, I asked who these people were, who wanted to rule the world.

Oh, didn't I know? Right here in mother Russia! Of course they had heard there were similar groups in America and in Europe. But in Russia this group was in power—and white power!

I looked around furtively. Wouldn't there be government agents listening in and having every one of us shot?

Captain Zaizeff noticed my furtive glance and laughed out loud. Then he looked intently at me as if searching my very soul while inquiring what big, strong, easy-going America would do after the war. Would she stay awake and become a real big brother to fellow nations so they could gain and hold their dream of peace? Would America retain and expand her power and become a leader? Or would she drop back into pre-war apathy, luxury-craze and splendid isolation? Would she scrap her arms program in favour of color television, new and better cars, refrigerators and pleasure boats?

I begin to understand Captain Zaizeff. I could see him now again as, a few months ago, he was walking down Strand with me, hatless in the bitter London fog, talking as eagerly as if the world's future depended on his words. I now realized it did. I began to understand the stock from which he came: a people yearning for the things I had taken for granted.

A Norwegian frigate took me west to Kirkenes, the Norwegian town closest to the Soviet border. A swab heaving my suitcase ashore announced, "Here's one for Captain Crofter." Thus our secret and secret code name was banded about. Did it matter, now that we had arrived? I still to this day wonder if it was all right to paint the codename in full-size letters on all our equipment.

The town was occupied by Soviet troops. How this happened was and still is a mystery to me. The town now provided a convenient base for us Norwegians intent on mopping up the German forces from the north southward.

This combined Russo-Norwegian venture was one of the smoothest of World War II. There was not even woman trouble. The Russians brought their own girls as nurses, cooks or ack-ack crews. The only extravagance was provided by a few acquisitive Russian soldiers walking the streets of Kirkenes, pointing guns at Norwegians in the streets and shouting,

"Tick-Tick!"

This form of begging for wristwatches was not appreciated by the tough men of Kirkenes who promptly shot forth powerful fists and flattened the uncouth beggars. I know of no case where the latter actually used their guns or achieved their objectives. They returned to their barracks especially complaining about Norwegian manners. Their superiors promptly put them in the clink. What they additionally did to these offenders I do not know. The practice stopped abruptly.

From the protected base of Kirkenes we fanned out over Finmark driving the Germans back. The takeover of Senja, a strategic island off the North Coast, became a classic. Lieutenant Godo went in with a platoon. The token-size German forces were foolish enough to offer resistance. Godo never cared much for the German invaders and this resistance gave him an excuse for being rough. He let three Germans survive to man the guard house and sentry posts when the relief ship came in. Godo and his men had them covered. In that way the relief troops were lured ashore and Lieutenant Godo indulged again.

He now guessed the enemy would send warships into various fields of the island so he marched his men to the anticipated points. He seemed to have a sixth sense as to timing.

The Germans, finding each fjord occupied by a platoon of men, concluded the island must be crawling with Norwegian soldiers and, considering their own dwindling supplies, gave up the required conquest.

Lieutenant Godo was not the first Norwegian using this ruse. It had been immortalised by Tordenskjold, a hero of the Middle Ages, who has later been claimed by the Danes, so this had better not be chronicled further.

In other areas the Germans tried to fight back. Once they had captured an old Lap, one of the original population of Northern Norway. The German propaganda ministry had informed them the Laps had been mistreated by the Norwegians and would gladly serve the Germans. The old man was asked to lead the Germans to Norwegian headquarters. A surprise attack was contemplated.

The idea had somehow been conveyed to the Germans that the "Laps" were not very bright. And now the German Colonel in charge of the expedition amused himself by muttering "Dummer Lap, dummer Lap," being sure the dumb Lap couldn't speak German. The word "dummer" (meaning 'dumb' followed by the male gender ending) is practically the same in Norwegian. The Lap understood too well but said nothing. In due time the German unit found itself between two lines of Norwegian troops. The Lap had sent a warning along a short route and had led the Germans along a detour into the trap. Now he laughed in the German Colonel's face,

"Dum Lap, Dum Lap, he he he!"

From our forward positions we made frequent trips back to base at Kirkenes. I used those occasions to take Russian language lessons from amiable Lieutenant Janovitch at Russian headquarters. I had brought a Russian language book with me.

I was soon to have plenty of time for Russian lessons. The 8th of May the radio in our tent somewhere on the Finnmark-Vidda announced the end of World War II. We had then retaken all of Finnmark, Norway's northern province. Meanwhile the Norwegian geurillas on Hardanoer-Vidda in the south had been so well-established that Eisenhower ordered the Germans in southern Norway to surrender directly to these geurillas. Rolf Eckhoff, who managed the radio communication with Eisenhower, told me it gave him quite a kick to see ponderous German generals scrape and bow before Norwegian youth with simple arm bands for insignia.

There may have been other surrender acts to Norwegian units but we in the north did not function in this manner. Our disappointment was mingled with no little pride that the Germans reportedly thought us too fierce to surrender to in comfort.

I went back to Kirkenes to await the screeching, long-winded halting and disassembling of a colossal war machine. It was a welcome rest, flavoured by language study.

Right in the middle of one lesson (held at Janovitch's office) the door burst open. A man in the uniform of a Russian Colonel stood in the doorway looking from Janovich to me as if we were among the ten most wanted.

"Oh, eh," said Janovitch, pale with fear, "This is Colonel Krasnoumoff, the new Commandant—and this is..."

Lieutenant Janovitch never finished. The Russian Colonel whipped the language book out of my hands as if it were the document that would seal my doom.

I was a fierce Norwegian, not trained to accept this sort of treatment, particularly not from a friend and ally. While looking the Colonel firmly in the eye I snatched the book back, then held it forth:

"If you please, Sir, I shall be glad and proud to show you this language book which happens to be mine, if you so request, with the courtesy due a friend and ally."

So the Russians, when peace broke, out, had sent a new Commandant of an entirely different hue to friend Norway. It boded no good. It gave ammunition to those who gloomily predicted the Russians would never leave Kirkenes. When, a few months after the war they did leave, this came as a pleasant surprise.

The Colonel accepted the proffered book without a word, turned on his heel, said to Janovitch,

"Follow me!"

And left, the pale Lieutenant trailing him.

The next day Lieutenant Janovitch came up to me smiling,

"The Commandant isn't angry!"

"Why should he be?"

"He wants to talk with you!"

"Who doesn't?"

"Could you come over this afternoon at four?"

"We'll see if we can crowd it in."

The new Commandant was all smiles when we were seated in his spacious office with glasses of vodka before us and a large sign on the wall saying in both Russian and Norwegian,

"The USSR greets its courageous Norwegian brothers-in-arms and encourages their fight to liberate their land from the Nazi invaders."

"We Russians," began the Commandant, "are very curious. Will you please forgive us? Now Lieutenant Janovitch tells me you have decided to go back to America. Why, may I ask, do you wish to go back to America?"

"Oh, that's an old decision. I had emigrated before the war. I just came back to fight the Nazis on my native soil. America has freedom, efficiency, challenges."

"Freedom!" he exploded. "Have you seen the freedom we have in the Soviet Union?"

His sudden ejaculation evoked the devil in me. The war had taught me to grab what was offered. I saw visions of a most exciting trip back to the US—at USSR expense! I saw no reason why this inquisitive Colonel should not pay for his curiosity by a free trip.

So I replied, "I haven't seen much. I would like to learn more. Why don't you arrange for my return trip to America via the Soviet Union—Moscow, Vladivastock, San Francisco?"

He laughed grimly.

"Haw haw, what wouldn't the capitalist press say, nay, scream! Mighty Russia interferes with little Norway, grabbing Norwegian officer, sending him to Russia!"

"It would be easy enough to refute that. And, really, you don't care, do you? Mighty Russia does not care about groundless rumours."

"We do care. But enough of that. What I should like to know is: Why don't you rather stay on here in Norway and see to it that Norway gets the right kind of government after the war?"

Now I was worried. Who did this Colonel think I was? What information or misinformation was he building on? Who had fabricated it? Who had access to it?

"What, exactly, do you mean by right kind of government?"

"Well," he made an expansive move, "you saw what the British did in Greece?"

What British acts in Greece the Commandant was referring to is anybody's guess. He had flashed some signals of the mystery of post-war Russia, forerunners of weird, ice cold gusts that I doubt Russians could define any better than we could. This didn't make me talkative. Our get-acquainted party ended on a sombre note.

Soon after this I accompanied Colonel Dahill of the Norwegian army on an air trip to Murmansk. The moment the engines stopped Russian officers came aboard and hauled the Colonel in triumph to a ding-dang feast in the Senior Officers' mess. I, a mere Captain, was left standing on the field in the bitter cold. Or was this a reminder for my being a poor sport at the Commandant's welcoming party? After half an hour a kind private came along and invited me to the soldiers' mess. We feasted on brown stale bread and coffee.

At about this time my friend, Theo Findahl, Berlin correspondent to *Aftenposten*, Norway's largest daily newspaper, made ready to leave Berlin for Oslo. The Russians told him he would have to go home via Moscow. Here he was questioned in a friendly but persistent manner: on which side would he be in the next war?

Next war? What were they talking about?

"Oh, come now! You, an informed newspaper man, know there will very soon be another war!"

"Where? Why? Between whom?"

"Between Russia and the United States, of course!"

Chapter 18

I Shall Call Him Finn

Front fighters are a proud lot; prouder still are the home front volunteers; proudest of all are those who hunt imaginary traitors. They come in every war and often between wars. They lack the taste or courage for genuine fighting so they fight the defenseless. They wield guns without the slightest danger of being shot back at. They jeopardize the work of established counter-espionage agencies, hamper and harass the real war effort apart from the agonizing suffering they bring to the some victims and their families.

One of my best friends had married a German girl just before World War II. I shall call him Finn and her Anna. She was from a fine old family whose home in Germany became a center of anti-Nazi talk and juicy stories about Hitler and his henchmen.

In due time an informer, a "provokateur," found his way into this home. First he listened, quietly, to what was said until he had gained a feel for the persons concerned. Then he contributed some stories himself and listened again to the reaction. The Germans, apprehensive of strangers, had not committed themselves and remained free while Finn, whose Norwegian education had failed to provide him with the subtler Continental diplomacy, promptly landed in a concentration camp. There, he did not kowtow to the guards and eventually found himself on death row.

Anna, his wife, knowing German ways and especially that SS guards, in spite of their professed contempt for the old aristocracy, usually fawned on the upper classes, made a point of visiting the camp, bringing baskets with champagne, expensive delicacies and, not the least, her own gracious company to the socially-starved guards. Her husband was removed from death row to a special cell built for distinguished guests temporarily detained. Soon after he was freed. The couple shook the fatherland's dust off their feet and departed for what they thought would be friendlier shores—Norway.

Upon landing in Oslo they took lodging at the Continental Hotel where they at once received a visit from two German Gestapo agents who suspected them of having brought secret papers and even samples of secret war gadgets with them from Germany. Their luggage and the entire room was searched. Finally Anna said,

"Why don't you look under the bed?"

They did and pulled out a formidable night pot, still a treasured feature in Norwegian hotels. As the Gestapo agent threw a sour glance at Anna, she added, "Look inside!"

What these Gestapo agents did not know was that Finn had brought secret papers and samples of new war gadgets from Germany, though sent from a cover address in Germany to a cover address in Norway. The items were never traced by the German authorities. Finn and later Anna continue to exploit their German connections and acquired valuable information with supporting evidence, all of which eventually ended up in England.

From Oslo the couple left for Finn's modest home in the mountains. It was a place of monumental natural beauty. It was also a place of bitter memories. At the beginning of the war in Norway, right after the Nazi invasion and before Finn's recent adventures in Germany, he had been at his father's hotel in Nybergsund when the King and Cabinet arrived there after having fled from Oslo. The whereabouts of a King and Cabinet is not easy to hide from enemy spies. The hotel was bombed though no one was hurt. The usual crop of hunters of fiction treasures looked for the 'leak'. Among the hunters was a formidable Swedish 'volunteer' wielding an oversized gun. There was Finn, son of the hotel owner, married to a German girl! The hero hunters looked no further. Finn nearly lost his life to trigger-happy no-risk hunters.

Finn and Anna had chosen to forget that unpleasant incident when they moved up to Finn's mountain home not far from his father's hotel. The local heroes had not forgotten. They barged in on the hapless couple like a swarm of hornets. The local police appear to have been hoodwinked by the traitor-hunters for Finn was taken to the local jail. The police chief could have acquired the true story of Finn simply by contacting the authorities in Oslo. Possibly he took Finn in to protect him from the mob. Anyway, Finn was subjected to endless questioning day after day, week after week on the premises, not by the regular police but by the same gun-wagging heroes who had bothered him before.

When I arrived in Oslo from Finmark after VE day, Rolf filled me in on Finn's fate. Rolf was the underground radio operator who have been communicating with Eisenhower's headquarters and had been authorized to accept the surrender of the German forces in Norway. Understandably he had been pretty busy. He now told me Finn's position had been deteriorating and he was in danger.

I told my superiors. They understood only too well. They had heard similar stories over and over again since coming back to Norway. I was awarded leave of absence and 20 gallons of gas. I wired the local police chief that I wanted to see him in five hours, on urgent business. Then we drove off in Rolf's car.

Arriving, we were told the police chief had just left town. He had delegated no one to see us. I was more sorry for him than angry. It was not difficult to imagine his dilemma, exposed to gun-wagging thugs hiding under the colours of the flag.

We found the local judge at home and explain to him the case in great detail, then asked if he had any additional information. He hadn't, but told us he could not take any action except on the advice of his chief of police.

We reminded him the police chief was not here to offer his advice.

"You'll have to come back," he said; then added pompously, "I never take a position contrary to my police chief."

I looked at Rolf. As one of the best informed leaders of the underground, this was his domain. He would have reports on this judge as on other Norwegian officials. He would know his war record, his degree of loyalty, his character.

Rolf looked at the judge and asked very quietly, as if in surprise,

"You are telling us, sir, that you never in your life took a position on your own, independently of your police chief or anybody else?"

The judge looked uncertainly from Rolf to me, back to Rolf, "I ..eh..did not exactly mean that. In fact, on two occasions I differed with my chief of police. "

In a voice cutting like a knife, Rolf replied, "Then let us hope, in the name of peace, that this will be your third such case. We have made the facts known to you. We have orders to bring Finn to Oslo tonight.

"With what authority are you speaking?"

The judge had raised his voice in anger. Rolf did not raise his voice when he answered,

"The captain, here, represents the total Allied Forces who battled and finally defeated the aggressors after millions of them had paid with their lives. His superiors sent him here."

"And Rolf here," said I, "fought on a still more dangerous front—the home front. He has just completed negotiations with Eisenhower's headquarters about surrender of the German forces in Norway to him and his colleagues in the underground."

"And Finn, who is wanted in Oslo tonight," continued Rolf, "fought for us on an even more dangerous front, in and out of Germany. The three of us represent the entire fighting forces of Allied might, which finally freed such as you, Mr. Judge. We represent the supreme authority in the world and in this country until a legal government will have been established. We have been requested by proper authority to carry out this present mission."

The judge blinked, "Ah...this is...quite serious then, I understand?"

"Quite serious, Mr. Judge. "

He gave us a paper ordering Finn's release.

"Will you go with us to the jail, Mr. Judge? "

"I...I am afraid I can't. I have other pressing business."

Six burly men guarding the jail were not quite ready to release their star prisoner on the strength of a piece of paper. I looked the six over. There was fury but also doubt in their faces. In two of the faces there was less fury, more doubt. They were regular policeman.

I addressed myself to the others, "What are you four men doing here?"

Their jaws dropped. One said, "We are deputy guards. The scoundrels on the inside need watching."

"What kind of police training did you have before you got this job?"

While they were thinking that one over, I went on, "Your two properly trained police colleagues here can certainly tell you what an order from a judge means, but apart from that you should know what the Allied Armed Services mean and what the Underground means (I pointed to Rolf.) We are here to take Finn with us to Oslo tonight. He has rendered exceptional service to our country, to us and to you. If we should be forced to use our weapons we shall do so. If we kill, it will be justified defence whereas if we are killed you will all hang for murder. Rolf will now open this lock…"

Rolf produced his locksmith kit with which he had burglarized so many exquisite German safes. Two of the guards drew near as to stop him. I directed my gun at their toes and said to Rolf, "Do you think, Rolf, I could manage to place bullets neatly between their toes like McCullan did in the Battle of the Bulge?"

"Well, Bryn, try! By all means try! You may never again have such a perfect case!"

The two deputies withdrew. The two regulars came forward and offered to open the lock.

"Thank you," said Rolf and stood back. "This lock is not too challenging anyway. Would have been a waste of good tools."

Finn had been a handsome lad with an open friendly face. The man who now entered, without having been told what it was all about, expecting perhaps another gruelling grilling—looked as if his face had been squeezed, shortened and distorted between a mischievous giant's thumb and forefinger. He threw his head from side to side, his eyes darting about nervously.

Then he noticed Rolf and myself. Slowly his face changed, grew to normal height, straightened itself. He leaped over to me and pounded my back.

The three of us walked away. One guard shouted, "Now wait a bit!"

Without slackening his pace Rolf turned his head, "Finn has waited long enough."

Chapter 19

Idiot's Delight

Behind the messes of battlefields and the litter left by occupation forces are subtler though no-less-painful wounds, hidden from most fighting men—damaged money structures, wrecked economies that may be repaired, if at all, only after years of gruelling toil. First of all a government commission must be named to assay the situation and propose a course of action.

At a meeting of Norwegian dignitaries in London in 1944, names were thrown into a hat for such a commission. Johann Nygaardsvoll, the Premier, tossed in my name.

"If that idiot is going to serve," hissed distinguished Dr. Conehead, "I quit."

There was drama and significance in Dr. Conehead's outburst. First, who but an idiot with delight in the dirty, thankless tasks of such a commission? Then also, the career that had earned me the idiot title must indeed have appeared idiotic to this distinguished economist. After having worked my way through more than 60 countries in capacities ranging from sheep station hand to economic planner, I returned home to ask questions. While asking my questions, I worked in a bank, with the government and as a technical consultant. My questions were: Why oh why did not even the most advanced nations manage to utilize more of their resources, their vast potentialities, their willing and eager workmen so that healthy outlets could be provided for the drive and ambitions of the many, rather than merely a few?

Naturally every engineer and scientist working with our potentials is haunted by the same questions. But these few eager beavers would have made hardly a dent were it not for the rising number of professional bankers and economists who have joined hands with engineers to bitterly fight those of their colleagues who still cling to a 19th century concept of a pie of unchanging size that we must share. The pie was not unchanging, even in the 19th century, but until then it appeared sufficiently possible for the parrot mind to swallow, and capitalist and socialist parrots alike did swallow it.

In this latter half of the 20th century it seems almost unnecessary to broach this matter. Many do now understand that our problem is not the sharing of a fixed-size pie but the building and garnishing up of vastly larger one. Yet, many powerful politicians and even some professional economists still stubbornly cling to past centuries though they are losing ground to more visionary colleagues such as Federal Reserve Board Chairman, Mariner Eccles; New York Federal Reserve Bank past president, Allen Sproule; Dr. Irving Fisher of Yale; Dr. John Philip Wernette of Ann Arbor (formerly of Harvard); the late "elder statesman" Bernard Baruch and so many more.

It is particularly interesting that the late President Kennedy began his tenure much as a fixed-size-pie man and matured during the stress and strain of presidential burdens and decision making to become an erudite realist and expansion advocate, thus offering his countrymen a more complete scope for their ambitions. His dramatic rise is lucidly recounted by Dr. Seymour Harris, Senior Counsel to the Secretary of the Treasury under Presidents Kennedy and Johnson, and himself a brilliant representative of economics based on scientific potentials.

In London in the '40s these concepts were less developed, less understood. The sparkling writings of A. deV. Leigh, then Secretary General of the London Chamber of Commerce, reached but a trickle. John Maynard Keynes' learned excursions into the inaccessible lingo 'economese' produced more enthusiasm than understanding within the ranks of economists trying to translate him, so that monocled Londoners quipped, "Where ten economists are gathered there are at least twelve contrasting opinions of which fourteen are Mr. Keynes'!"

Norway's distinguished economist may thus have been fully justified in calling me an idiot at the time. The Prime Minister's response was curt, "Good, Dr. Conehead; that rids us of you."

Many factors contributed to his choice. A bloated, war-torn economy can only rise from the ruins through a flexible money policy, temporarily inflationary if need be, while the same-size-pie men know nothing better than cutting down the money supply to fit a pie that was already tragically undersized to begin with. Growth may thus be permanently stunted.

The Prime Minister might have had other reasons as well. A man constantly pressed for results; a man haunted by want and suffering around him, may find small comfort in advisors telling him only that nothing can be done. From ivory towers of age-old teachings and concepts, solemn voices boom on him about wicked politicians violating sacred laws (laws all constructed by that fertile imagination of our jittery minds) adding that if government would not interfere (leaving others to do the interfering) then, ah—all would be well!

Against such an appealing philosophy a far-travelling scientist-engineer brought promise of betterment, held out a concept of bold action, of trial and error rather than theories and laws.

My concluding minority report was supported by Dr. Ragnar Frisch of Oslo, outstanding econometrist and expansionist.

With Frisch in my corner I felt I could rightfully depart for the USA. He would defend my report better than I could. I have been told it was accepted and acted upon by the Norwegian Congress. But to what extent was it accepted and how was it acted upon?

I confess blushingly that I do not know. Moreover, I was emphatically warned that I ought to have made it my business to know and to keep in touch.

When I told the Prime Minister I considered my job done and was returning to America, he said,

"Your job is less than half done. Your very special career makes you an advisor I should like to have had around. You put adventure before duty. You were playing at the front lines when you should have stayed with us in London. Now you are reaching for the great American dream rather than carrying through what you have begun:

to provide Norway with a proper money situation. As you say, Dr. Frisch may do better than you but that is not for you to decide. You are both needed here."

He looked at me, then continued:

"I am not talking to you as a school master but as a repentant sinner. Once I, too, ran away to big, adventurous America. I was a strong lad so they gave me heavy logs to carry. That was the adventure."

I was surprised and disappointed. He had sailed to America as a lad and gone to work as a lumberjack, thus filling a need in America's great, pulsating life. Wasn't that his intent—to fill a need? Or did this otherwise bright and alert man mean to blame a whole nation for his own career, for not finding him a job more to his liking?

His next words provided an answer:

"You have built up a name for yourself in Norway. If you had stayed and completed your work here you would have been welcomed in America on a higher level. If you go now you'll be a lumberjack or the equivalent. This is not a criticism of America, only of you. Remember, Dr. Conehead called you an idiot. His reasons were invalid. But think about the term anyway, think hard before you leave."

How does one react to advice from a Prime Minister? At least one may think about it. Having thought long and hard, I have excuses: toiling with the Norse economy before the war, I had discovered our far-from-self-sustaining nation could do little without allies. One ally everybody wanted: America. I had visions not merely of a military alliance but a close economic cooperation. I went to America for many various purposes some of which were not even clear to myself. One, at least, was clear. I talked to America's bankers, economists, money men about the problems we had in Norway. Everyone was most responsive. In Washington, DC, a man high in the government told me after a long, rewarding exchange of ideas,

"I say, we here in Washington, DC, should look more around the world for bright ideas. They are not all here in this little town!"

While the response in the world of economics has been spectacular, though impersonal, my military experience, on the other hand, was tried out for size for a job. A group of American officers thought enough of me to recommend me to the then-head of psychological warfare. We had an hour's amiable chat. Then the official said,

"It has been nice talking to you. As you know, this unit never hires immigrant citizens; not because we don't trust you, but because you are biased."

Well, that statement couldn't be disputed for who isn't biased? However, there are degrees of harm ensuing from various forms of bias and perhaps the worst may be the bias of ignorance. Americans are now involved all around the world but hardly ever do we make use of the competence of immigrants originating in the area in question. If we did use this important and specifically American privilege in our work, American foreign missions would become the envy of the world. Upholders of the American dream, such as I, have the right and the duty to remind the natives (of America) of their prerogatives and potentialities so that more may reach the goals they set.

The only thing that now remains to be said is that American air crews made possible my work on the Norwegian Monetary Commission. They flew me from the Western Front to London at moments' notices every time there was a meeting, thus moving my lowly body and lowlier mind from the cares and dares of a frontal war to the subtler war of nerves and arguments and to the vulnerable missile target that was our London of that day. Thus I learned again that you can't do anything anywhere in the world these days without the help of those generous and over-efficient (you're darn-tootin') AmOricans!

Chapter 20

Peace Strikes

The august galaxy of authors and philosophers who verbalise the theme of war or peace appear to have overlooked the essential feature of travel and of food.

To the serviceman in war, it is free. As soon as peace strikes and he is in mufti again, woe unto him if he still tries to wangle a ride or a meal!

The bitter lessons I have learned from such efforts, from freeloading and aerial hitchhikings, are now offered to the public for the first time as a warning and uplift. Free rides or meals do not pay. Buy a ticket and support your friendly carrier! Stay in three-star hotels!

There was that holy ashram at Rishikesh where we slept on beds of woven weeds and feasted on fresh mango, olives, wild fern, milk from sacred cows, without paying a cent—until our thoughtless curiosity forced us to inquire into the economy of such an organization. Only then where we offered the opportunity of helping with a little offering—far beyond what a hotel would have cost.

There was that trip I undertook to see the majestic Indonesian volcano, Krakatoa, or what was left of it, by signing on as a deckhand on the Emma Bakke. When the coveted volcano was in view, I was on my back in the bilge tunnel scraping flakes of old paint off the tunnel ceiling. This added colour interest to my face, already purple with claustrophobia, but did nothing to fulfil the purpose of my trip.

Worst of all, I think, was my guest ride from Los Angeles to—supposedly—New York which ended in Spain from where I had to return to New York via Oslo at the cost of more than twice that of a ticket from Los Angeles to New York, not to mention a waste of time.

Dizzy from hooting horns, off-key rattlings of empty cans suspended behind speeding cars and from the onslaught of girls who were kissing everybody, I realized vaguely that this was PEACE, Hollywood style. It was August 14, 1945.

I had been on my way from the European to the Pacific theatre of war when the hurricane hit me. Now where was I? No more theaters! No more free travel! Simply peace, that was all, back to the peace of New York City—hooting horns, off-key rattlings, and all.

New York City? That was 3000 miles away. A rapid survey of air space divulged acute shortage. Everything was booked for weeks ahead.

Peace or no peace, plans began to seethe through my vagrant soul, plans for one more free ride.

In the lobby of the Douglas Aircraft Company the receptionist looked me over with that receptionist look, promising she would do anything for me—well, almost anything. I asked for Malcolm Sturgis.

Well (double smile), where in the plant did Mr. Sturgis work?

I shook my head, flushed awkwardly, turned as if to leave. There is nothing more pathetic than a frustrated back. The receptionist became professionally aroused. She insisted she would find Malcolm Sturgis. The do-it-or-die spirit of the war was still hers.

I now revealed that Malcolm had been command pilot on a bombing mission into the Ruhr on which I humbly served. This doubled her determination. I said I thought he was now working at Douglas. I found it unnecessary to divulge that I had no particular foundation for such an assumption. An officer and gentleman, even a past one, never tells a lie but neither is there any need to revel in unsolicited truth. I did let it be known that all I had wanted Mr. Sturgis for in the first place was to have him help me get a ride to New York and since I thought he worked here.

The receptionist's eyes now reflected the gleam of the command pilot. Malcolm Sturgis was necessary no longer! She picked up the telephone.

The amazing effect came only moments later: a Prince Charming emerged from the swinging door as if jet-propelled (a premature civilian locomotion at that time.) He steered for the receptionist who waved her hand and directed him to me.

"My government is proud," he bowed, "to have you as a guest on our plane."

The prince was a Spanish co-pilot who, with an American crew including pilot, was to take a plane just bought by the Franco government back to Spain. I reached for my wallet."

"No, no," the prince waved his slender hands. "Only you must sign a paper that you will not sue us."

"Certainly," I agreed, "but why would I ever want to sue?"

He laughed. "It is one of those things—in case you fell out and got killed, for example."

Then he chuckled to himself realizing the improbability of a dead man suing his government.

My new command pilot switched back to receptionist, powdered her nose and stroked back her hair, just in time to show herself at her best when the co-pilot prince turned his smile upon her. Oh, that a woman would ever powder her nose for me!

The prince turned to me again. "A spirit like the old Spanish conquistadores!" he exclaimed with repeated bows of appreciation. Then he left for final preparations. While I waited, people from the shops, the stores, the drafting rooms, the supervisors' cubicles, came out and took a quick and bashful gander at the G.I. who had wangled a ride in the spirit of the old Spanish conquistadores.

The telephone rang. The receptionist smiled into the receiver. Patting her hair, she turned to me. "Sir," she cooed, "can you leave in two hours?"

I was speechless, realizing this time it was for me she had patted her hair.

The Big Bear Mountains nodded to us and the Continental Divide winked at us condoning my trip and my having made intelligent use of the available amenities of a high civilization.

There was soup over New York, the kind of soup the earthbound call fog. Commercial airlines were grounded but we had a schedule to meet. We were the only craft in the soup. Circling over Idlewild, burning fuel, we had to make a decision. There was no hole so we just headed down through the thick soup. The first sign of approaching land was a flower pot on a ledge of a roof in Flushing. We must've touched it, for the pot rocked two and fro, but didn't topple. We shoved in for a perfect landing. Having won the battle of the flower pot, I felt so elated I cut some paper medals out of my orders to transfer to the Pacific Theatre and decorated the entire crew. With this accomplished, I was about to make my exit. The consternation on their faces warned me that exit now would be unconquistadorish. The flight engineer put it in words:

"Our gallant Mr. Hitchhiker, you have been so much with us. You brought us luck. You can't break up the team now. Come with us to Spain!"

I tried a mild protest but I was fresh out of the Services. In the Services whatever comes, you never break up the team.

There was sunshine in Madrid and it was gently warm. The streets were adorned with proud beauties and the gallant Spaniards did not keep it a secret but dutifully complemented the passing ladies, "A, Señorita, you are delightfully rounded!"

The recipients of the compliments gracefully smiled their appreciation. While contemplating the merits of the Spanish beauties I found it hard to decide whether and when to stop being a conquistador and return to the New York version. I kept comparing the rounded contours with my roundabout ways and comforted myself with the oft-heard truism that the most attractive route between two points is not always the straight line. In addition, I visited sailors' dens where one may learn of the adventurers who have jumped ship and left vacancies for such as I. Sailors may be the only remaining representatives of really free enterprise.

I learned that two salts had just jumped a ship bound for Oslo. That Oslo was even further from New York than Madrid was an annoying detail which, however, I could not bother with for the present.

And also I was further detained by luxurious living at the taxpayers' expense. My story would be incomplete without confession on this point, however painful.

The indiscretion was committed in Stortinget, the Congress or parliament building in Oslo, the western part of which is a stone monster, obviously a contemporary of Noah's ark while the eastern part is the more recent addition that makes modern romanticists rave and rant about efficiency, and the spirit of the West.

The first victims of this efficiency and this spirit are the Norwegian congressmen or "Stortingsmen" who must hang their hats in a sinister cell in the old building which obviously housed the doomed political opponents of bygone kings—then if constituents or nature beckons, they must proceed by secret winding stairs and wooden scaffolds to the new building. There, if nature were the beckoner, contraptions await them which have all the earmarks of the spirit of the West including warm-air hand driers and boisterously rotating shoe shiners, a left one for black shoes; a right one for the brownies.

A point of interest is that these facilities are by no means reserved for the duly elected ones, but offer their amenities free to any traveller bold enough to penetrate into these holiest of holies.

My undoing was the sit-down telephone. This was in a booth that might be called a boudoir since it was done in pink and light blue with a chair in strawberry, too spacious to be a booth yet small enough to have the cosy touch of a ladies' retiring room. Here any man without a conscience or even with budding criminal tendencies can sit down, stretch his legs, leisurely pull out of his pocket his telephone list and without the slightest expense to himself proceed to communicate. For his guidance there were printed directions; dial nine, wait for the summing tone, then proceed to dial your number.

These facilities of the Stortinget are doubly tempting in the austere Métropole of Oslo, for the lobbies of the better Oslo hotels do not lend themselves so readily as do American hotel lobbies to family reunions, business conferences, hot dates or gossip parties for people who never registered nor consumed anything at these hotels.

For students of history the Stortinget telephone boudoir offers an inspiring setting. Relaxed in the strawberry chair, they may meditate upon the gay old Vikings slaying each other as a mutual favour so they could go to Valhalla, the heaven for good Vikings or, when they tired of this, they took trips to the French and English coast, burned down houses and brought worthy maidens back with them. Or the student may view the less distant past when the three Scandinavian nations were so well organized they could battle each other on a national scale. Again he may look in on the German occupation of World War II when the Nazis made their headquarters—or rather one of a score of headquarters—in the Stortinget. Then, the great Terboven haunted these premises—great in both rank and sin—but physically so small and unattractive that even the German top Army Commander never referred to him in other terms than "that little stinker."

Terboven was an impetuous little man with the insistent curiosity of a terrier and one day, the story goes, he decided to investigate more thoroughly the ins and outs of the mysterious Stortinget. They could hear him stomping up and down winding iron stairs, in and out of ancient secret doors. After several hours of this he began to curse and swear. Obviously he had lost his way. His cronies made some token effort to locate him but they were not too eager. If the little stinker got lost for good—well, good riddance! So, the venerable old building that housed the ghosts of Vikings and kings now had to suffer the disgrace of housing the ghost of Terboven who had ordered the torture of thousands of Norwegian patriots. Night watchmen who have business in the old building late at night or in the early hours tell of the sound of footsteps searching, always searching; the fateful outcome of another free journey.

No wonder the temptation to stay overnight became almost irresistible. For such a purpose there are most sumptuous sofas placed along the corridors in the new part of the building. They have been designed to soften the moods of irate voters coming to complain to their Stortingsmenn. The Stortingman just deposits the visitor into one of these fanciful fluffs whereupon he sinks down and down into fleecy forgetfulness.

The temperature is moderate and one can safely sleep in this luxury without any covering other than the clothing he walks in. It has been whispered though, that some bring blankets and sheets and the snobs even their toothbrushes!

One bold constituent felt so at home in Stortinget that he phoned from his Congressman's chambers to the Grand Hotel across the street and ordered a smorgasbord sent up. When the bill later arrived for the congressman he decided, after having recovered from the shock, to pay. After all, a constituent well fed would cast a sure ballot.

Among us others there was agreement that this particular constituent had gone beyond the line of demarkation for honest thieves.

Being neither a Stortingsman nor an unscrupulous constituent, I had to continue on to New York and my work. I was offered a job on a ship working my way back to Los Angeles but this posed the prospect of returning to that charming Douglas receptionist to ask for another ride because the first one had brought me a bit too far. This I couldn't stomach. So I settled for a state room on the MS Oslofjord at a little better than twice the cost of going from Los Angeles to New York.

After an exhaustive search in New York City, in the lower 60s of Manhattan I located an ancient brownstone house which reeked of ghosts. I installed myself hopefully and was encouraged by gargantuan monstrosities oil-painted on entire walls.

Fathom my delight when, at the stroke of midnight, a noise as of hooting horns and rattling cans emanated from the basement. Were these the spirits of peace—New York style?

I ran down the stairs, prepared for a boy-meets-ghost, a worthy epitaph to an almost all-nation war. There was a whiff of breath past my nose. Two pairs of coat tails streaked up the stairs loaded with my host's and my own treasures. Surely the New York ghosts were younger than those of Stortinget and more acquisitive and faster moving.

Epilogue

Yes it took all of this, and more, to win and to see and feel that we had won. We had won the respect and allegiance of two brilliant though over-ambitious enemies, Germany and Japan. We had swapped a wicked past for a better present and a promising future. We can afford to stop worrying now, whether some people were once Nazis or Asian co-prosperity proponents. These, like all of us, have climbed out of the past into a present and future.

So didn't this remarkable war enoble all of us? The airmen and the infantry? The burglars and the Robin Hoods? The Germans and the Japanese? Russians and Norwegians? The English? Dutch? The French and the Belgians? Even us Americans? The black, white, yellow and the brown? The soul behind the color?

I wonder. In the night I hear Count Stauffenberg's screams as his left leg is torn from his body, while high-placed Americans stuff themselves at a lavish meal after rejecting the appeal to help get rid of a rascal, saying with salve, "The Germans must be beaten so they know it." Germans knew better than some Americans who ought to be beaten.

Appendix

In his 1970's book, *Every Willing Hand*, Shamcher outlined an economic plan for full employment and its beneficial effects on all aspects of western life at that time to secure a safe future. As he addressed once again some of the experiences outlined in *A Sufi Went to War*, this chapter is included here for comparision.

War (from *Every Willing Hand*)

The Nazi occupiers tried to force Norwegian youth to fight its Russian allies during World War II. They would have succeeded were it not that the Americans had kept their powder dry and threw out the Nazis. Worse, if Hitler had not been defeated by war, he would today have been running the world, based on nuclear power, and deciding where and for what every young man should fight and die. And some of my sincere, though ignorant American friends are appalled that I make my living building torpedoes, keeping America continuously prepared!

I was 44 when World War II started, considered too old to fight. I had to browbeat my way into the armed forces. In time, with British Intelligence and escaped German officers, we made detailed plans for kidnapping Hitler and ending the war early in 1944. The British were delighted. Franklin Roosevelt, at a safer distance from the front, turned us down, "The Germans must be beaten so they know it." If we, assigned to this mission, who had thus put our lives on the line, may be permitted a word, it is this: There are times when the horrors of war must be accepted to prevent greater horrors. I have met mutilated veterans and shuddered, "There, but for the grace of God, go I," but even these tell me they would have done it again.

In addition, the nation's economy ran smoother, the living standard soared and somber warnings that we would be ruined in the future came to naught, for the sacred goal of winning welded us into efficient working units so we put out ample goodies in addition to munitions. We were close together. All talents were sought and used. We did not waste away our lives in unemployment. While some of us fought on the outside, the nation's insides were warm, healthy and compassionate.

This reminded us that we had been unable in peace time to grasp the urgent needs that ought to have kept us all as busy as the more obvious need of winning a war.

The smoothly-running economy made the war look attractive, to the non-combatants at least, with the consequence that World War II, for example, was prolonged far beyond its useful life. This writer was involved, as a linguist, soldier and adventurer, in the first German approaches to Allied quarters. The war was not old when high-placed Germans offered to help dispose of the Hitler gang and establish a new cooperative German government. There was every reason to believe in their sincerity, as well as their ability to carry out their plans. Never more than 44% of the German people had ever voted for Hitler; most years much less. He had beaten and murdered his way to power in spite of the 56%, or most, who opposed him. He never represented the German people.

Among those who favored the plans of the German dissidents were Allan Dulles, at that time only a minor U.S. intelligence operator who could not yet swing the minds of Premiers and Presidents; Trevor Roper, British historian and intelligence operator, and others in the thick of action though thin in power. Platitudes, such as "We must beat the Germans so they know it," were countered by British General J. F. Fuller, "The 56% majority of Germans don't need that lesson. The rest cannot be taught and do not matter."

Greater names had their way, ignoring General Fuller, and have weighing on their conscience (if such exists after death?), millions of American, British and continental lives, among which the very Germans who could make the post-war years worthy of the sacrifices.

What, in the scheme of things, caused the emergence of a Hitler gang and its wars? A short-circuit in the current that feels and knows that every living being represents the universe. Hitler, near-sighted, fancied his limited person and his friends represented it against others who did not. But how could this unholy mixture of imagination, lies and hypocricies be accepted by such a substantial part of a great people? Because of intolerable pressure brought about by clumsy, inoperable economic sanctions.

Once launched, Hitler's thrusts at first were more successful than even he had expected, for none of his powerful neighbors lifted a hand to defend the victims. Atrocious crimes were committed against people and races while the world sat still in the name of PEACE, which from then on became a dirty word and still may be.

One by one, we finally awoke and saw that there was something greater than peace, morally and practically greater and more necessary. That morally and practically greater thing was WAR.

We learned that war itself is neither wrong nor necessarily right. What is wrong is that we start wars too late and carry them on too long.

The Korean war, predictable to the wary, came as an unpleasant surprise to those American leaders who had sent Phillip Jessup, a distinguished John Hopkins scholar, to East Asia, ostensibly on a "fact-finding" mission. Equally distinguished foreign service officers had collected facts for centuries in those same areas, so nobody swallowed this version of the mission. I happened to be on a lower level, partly self-inflicted mission in the same area at this same time and the pretensions of Jessup's mission so galled me that I deposited, with a friend in the Embassy of Tokyo, a less than scholarly treatise on the subject of FACTS, postulating that in international relations, particularly, facts are not "found" but made. Dr. Jessup is rumoured to have chuckled over it.

So, we waited for the real purpose of Jessup's visit to be revealed. It was. In the first spot of his landing, and thereafter in every following place, he said, with variations, that Asia must not expect from the United States a participation or an aid program in any way comparable to our European commitments. This was Dr. Jessup's mission: Not to find a fact but to produce one. What he produced was the Korean War. This may not have been his explicit purpose, nor the purpose of those who sent him. But our distinguished North Korean, Chinese and Russian counterparts interpreted to the best of their ability these statements, then staged the invasion of South Korea on the apparently well-founded belief that the United States would not interfere.

My own appearance in Japan at Christmas 1949 was not solely to take part in General MacArthur's perennial New Year Party at the Imperial Hotel, although this was worth the trip all by itself, for you were permitted and even urged to hug and kiss the entire complement of American womanhood in the area from age eighty down to sixteen, at midnight sharp, and the Geishas to boot. In addition, I had been commissioned by a friend to retrieve about a $100,000 worth of gold dust deposited by a fugitive from the Bolsheviks near Blagovaschensk on the river Amur. My friend had also involved U.S. intelligence. This project held no treasure hunt charm for me; for if I survived at all there would be nothing left for me after the Russians had taken their share, and my friend what he considered his. But it was as good an excuse as any for going in and seeing what the Russkies were up to—a fact-finding mission after all?

How far up the MacArthur hierarchy my plan was supported I do not know, but with the ranks it was a shoe-in. All information that could be obtained was badly needed. But the local representative of the State Department said no, and so probably saved my life, though was it worth saving?

So the Korean war came along without my assistance. It took thousands of American and Korean lives to prove that America, as a whole, did not share the sentiments of those appointed officials who sent Dr. Jessup on his fact-producing mission. The United States, a giant rider straddling Europe and Asia, can never ignore the plight of either.

My Tokyo friends told me that while I could not enter the Soviet Union from Japan, there was no objection to my entering from any other point. So, I had the most cordial encounter with Ivanshenko in Hong Kong, officially Russian Trade Commissioner, actually one of the eminences behind the vast and secret Russian gold. He told me a $100,000 worth was like a grain of sand compared to Russia's actual holdings. But this grain of sand, I countered, might nevertheless become of some interest to certain Russians and Americans? Seeing Ivanshenko's cold stare. I quickly emptied my glass of vodka and sank deeply into the armchair trying to become invisible.

I made a daring thrust as far as Chungking, China's ancient capital, where I happened to see Chiang Kai-Shek, long since rumored to be in Taiwan, standing very erect in a luxurious overcoat, back-slapping and well-wishing his associates, then emplaning for Taiwan; an insouciant, unworried target for red snipers. Whatever his politics, the old man displayed regal courage.

Further penetration became impossible. Reluctantly I had to backtrack, using the last exiting missionary plane, the St. Paul, outrageously overloaded, a pile of furniture and trunks in the middle of the floor upon which the children played mountaineers, yelling their "whoopees" while the missionaries prayed earnestly that the plane would lift, which it did, obligingly, knocking two telephone poles in the noble effort.

The Korean War brought us in close touch with long-term torture as a government policy. A village chief not yet proven, merely being suspected of being anti-red friend-of-yanks would be strung up and slowly tortured through weeks. His dead body would continue to hang there until the stink would duly have impressed upon all what happens if you don't play ball. Many of our boys seeing this, fought more fiercely, hoping to produce a impression of their own. But some worried whether this zeal might be exposed to the same kind of torture, which might eat away their enthusiasm.

There was another creeping fear: That our troops might become brutalized, infected with this same disregard for fellow-humans. This, in addition to strategic and tactical reasons, was why all our military men became convinced we must never again become involved in a land war in Asia. General Ridgeway, who knew the ins and outs of the Korean War was a major spokesman for this view, along with General Gavin. If the so-called "military mind" could have prevailed, we might not have been in Vietnam at all, even though visible and invisible pressure from less knowledgeable Presidents and their entourages caused many officers to condone our land war in Vietnam.

The "military mind" syndrome was indulged in even by such an intellect as Jawaharlal Nehru. He used the expression when we talked about President Eisenhower. Later, when he had seen and talked to him, he admitted he had been mistaken. "I have never met a man more genuinely concerned with peace." A military man, with experience in his ghoulish line, knows the horrors of war and that all means must be employed to avoid it.

As for myself, hailing from Norway, which has not been attacked since the Atlantic Pact was signed because, I believe, the

U.S. dropped hints it would go to war if Norway was invaded, I wondered if the Korean War would have happened at all if the U.S. instead of shouting that Asia would have to take care of itself, had said, as in the case of Norway, that an attack would be squarely met.

In Asia, in addition, there is China. What do we know of China? More than anyone else in the Western World. Apart from all our immigrants from China and citizens of Chinese descent, the U.S. has more people who know and understand China than any other nation. Through such people, the Mainland Chinese government has made probings through the years. Forced by an irate section of the citizenry, our government has remained aloof and non-committal until now, finally, there has been a coming-together.

The priceless benefit of the Vietnam War has been the revelation it provided of our volatile emotions and stunted thought patterns, upon which might possibly follow a sobering process. Here an over- sized half of the nation pompously proclaimed that all we did was thoughtlessly intrude into a domestic quarrel at a fabulous price in lives and billions. The undersized rest of us thought we had honestly tried to save a striving democracy from cruel and reactionary red bullies.

The former say: Who could connect the term "bully" with good old Ho Chi Minh's saintly face with the long, silky beard? My French friends told me he sold his own commie friends (those he didn't like) to the French secret police and their torture chambers. Senior Congressperson Frances Bolton asked me in the sixties what to do about requests for vast increases in our troops to Vietnam. I said I would love to have helped my South Vietnamese friends, possibly by some intelligence action or naval operations; but more land forces in Vietnam would not help, would destroy more than we could build. I have compassion for my countrymen who had to make those fateful decisions, though I wonder why they did not listen to senior Generals Ridgeway and Gavin, the misunderstood and abused "military minds".

We might have "won" in Vietnam, by conducting the war on military principles rather than as a parlor game, but what would be the sense of destroying a country and its future livability just because a cruel band had ruled and mistreated its citizens and threatened others? No secure haven would have been created, just wastelands, more hate and additional bloodbaths.

All this we learned in or from Vietnam, though at a price. Some of us, who found the facts too hard to face, took refuge in drugs. This was also correctly foreseen by our so unappreciated "military minds" who are now busy controlling and reversing this trend, incidentally just a fraction of the nation's alcohol problem.

While hardly a word has been heard in this country about Ho Chi Minh, this former CIA hireling, and what he has cost our country in lives and billions, former President Thieu of South Vietnam who headed a government of our own creation, has been continuously misrepresented and mistreated by "important", ignorant and infantile writers. May we learn from this?

War is destruction, though occasionally it fosters greatness. Mucius Scaevola, a Roman patriot, volunteered to kill Lars Porsena who was besieging Rome, just like modern CIA agents today volunteer to risk death and torture to protect us. Mucius was caught and sentenced to be burned alive. Smilingly, he placed his right hand into a coal fire until it was burned to a crisp. This is why he was later called Scaevola, the lefthanded one. Lars was so impressed, he freed Mucius and gave up the siege.

In Norway, during the Nazi occupation, I met men who had been repeatedly tortured, in a way few ever survived, to make them reveal names of the underground. They were treated to boiling enemas that seemed to burn out their insides.

"How can you stand it?"

"There comes a time when you don't care any longer what happens to you. You know only one thing: You are not going to give."

"What about the pain?"

"The pain I first felt was half fear, fear of death. I don't fear death any more, so I feel only half the pain. It is bearable."

Such sentiment may not make sense to one who is thrown into a war he does not understand or can't believe in. But a volunteer who knows he defends his country, his ideal, sees such moments as pinnacles of achievement. They are. To him, war lifts him above his human limitations to touch his Creator.

The many more, whom war does not lift, to whom war is unacceptable cruelty, what hope can they be given? No promise of eternal peace, only the prospect that through diligent study of man in all parts of the world, we may reach an insight that will permit us to diminish causes of major wars and eventually substitute police functions.

First of all, our present volatile "deterrent" system can be changed. One contemplated alternative was presented in Foreign Affairs, January 1973, by Fred Charles Ikle, former professor of political science at MIT and recently closely connected with weapons systems and strategy.

Dr. Ikle hopes to eliminate the vulnerability of our strategic arms to surprise attack and thus break the vicious circles: That they must be ready for prompt launching because they are vulnerable, and they are vulnerable because they must be ready. Weapons incapable of quick launching are less suitable for surprise; and against truly invulnerable nuclear armaments, surprise would have lost its purpose. For example, he proposes, arms hidden deeply underground, which could be launched only through weeks or months, would permit second thoughts, change of mind when warranted, over-riding panic decisions or correcting faulty messages. This, he admits, seems like a small step, but may be a beginning that might well save this globe from destruction.

Careful techno-socio-psychologic studies must precede such a step. Is it not possible, for example, that an enemy knowing it would take weeks or months before retaliation could strike would go ahead with his attack, believing he could counter the counter attack by some means when given that much time? And might he not be right? An adventurous or even erratic bossman might well gamble. But the idea is worth serious consideration.

Now the sixty-nine billion dollar question: What causes wars? As for World War II, the answer was easy: Hitler. But why did such a character gain power in Germany? What level of despair caused a great people to listen to his ravings?

The German economy was out-of-kilter. Germans starved. The payments imposed on Germany after World War I were to be made, not in German goods exported to the Allies, the only way in which any nation can pay. No, the payments were to be made in dollars and other non-German currency. How could Germany obtain dollars? Only by selling German goods in the States. But we refused to let them do that. We were afraid this would increase our own unemployment. We tried, like other Western nations, to maintain what we called a "favorable" trade balance, meaning to sell for more than we bought. The only way any one can maintain such a "favorable" balance is for others to have an unfavorable one. On this self-destructing principle has the world economy operated—or misoperated, and still does.

About the Author

Bryn Beorse (Shamcher) (1896-1980) was the author of many non-fiction books, novels and articles, covering topics of energy, economics, full employment, and global awareness as well as yoga and Sufism.

Born in Norway, he worked and travelled in over 65 countries in his lifetime, and he eventually settled in the United States. Fluent in several languages, his comprehensive worldview included the inner meditative life as well as the accomplishment of life in the world.

Sent on a UN economic mission to Tunisia in the 1960's, helping to rebuild the Norwegian economy after WWII, Beorse also spent time in exploration, travelling to the Kumbha Mela in India, living as a beach bum in the dunes of Oceano, and going to China at the time of the revolution. A spy in WWII, he was part of the plot to kidnap Hitler. An advocate of the giro-credit economic system, he spoke out against the stagnation of hierarchical organization.

An accomplished yogi and Sufi, Shamcher was instrumental in developing Sufi centers throughout the world, in the tradition of Inayat Khan. He devoted the last years of his life once again to promoting OTEC, Ocean Thermal Energy Conversion, the source of benign solar power from the sea.

Subscribe to the Shamcher Bulletin newsletter at shamcher.substack.com

www.ingramcontent.com/pod-product-compliance
Lightning Source LLC
Chambersburg PA
CBHW071118160426
43196CB00013B/2615